To! Pamph

LEGACY MINDED MEN

UNDERSTANDING THE SECRETS OF THEIR HEARTS

DR. D. ROBERT KENNEDY

ISBN: 978-1-7321890-9-6

Legacy Seminars LLC

11503 Belvidere Road

Bowie, MD 20721

legacyseminars41@gmail.com

website: www.thelegacyseminars.com

The pertinent information gathered in this collection by Dr. D. Robert Kennedy, is directed to men. There is no question that the author is a prolific writer who is most effective in conveying his thoughts to challenge any man who will read and listen. Reading the collection has greatly stimulated me, and I believe it will stimulate all who will receive it with an open heart. - Mr. Maurice Jarvis, Prayer Support Leader, Orange, New Jersey.

Legacy Minded Men is a must read for anyone interested in understanding what character traits make men of character and integrity. Dr. D. Robert Kennedy puts forward many compelling ideas that challenge men to be conscious of their character in a world so little concerned with character today. –Marcellus T. Robinson, D.Min.

Director of Stewardship/Philanthropy/Trust Services

Allegheny East Conference Corporation of Seventh-day Adventists

Legacy Minded Men is a resource that shows how men in the contemporary culture impart their legacy for generations to come. It gives a special focus to the transference of faith. Many family life educators argue that men represent the most consistent, and arguably the most critical agents upon the 3rdand 4thgenerations in the transference of any faith. In this vein, I am thankful that Dr. D. Robert Kennedy made faith a central component of these reflections. To me, it is a blessing for men to read.- Augustus Lawrence, D. Min. Family Ministries Director, South England Conference of SDA, 25 St Johns Road, Watford, WD17 1PZ.

As you read *Legacy Minded Men*, take time to reflect on the situations and principles presented and how you may incorporate positive changes into your life. Continuous improvement of our mental, emotional and spiritual life is an ongoing process. Read this book. Dog-ear pages and highlight areas that resonate with you personally. It will serve as a blessing to your life's journey! - Clairmont J. Barnes, Jr., Springfield, VA., *Just for Men* prayer call group. Emmanuel Worship Center.

The clarion call has sounded forth for men to consider the legacy that is passed on to the generations that will live after we are long gone. Nobody does it better than Dr Kennedy. Practically interwoven with a degree of delicate intensity in this enlightening work are words which passionately convey the essence of godly character, respect, trust, integrity, honesty... these words are legacies that we owe society and the Kingdom of God. Once again must read masterpiece and an insightful read! -

George Kumi, Ministerial Director, North England Conference of Seventh-day Adventist. 22 Zulla Road Nottingham Nottinghamshire NG3 5DB.

FOREWORD

Dr. D. Robert Kennedy, offers this collection of wisdom directed to men, expressed with the insight of someone who knows how men think. He is seeking to help men make effective decisions to shape their lives for eternity. I am especially blessed to have the opportunity of benefitting from his multiple decades of service in multiple-dimensional ministry within the United States and the church around the world. The title of this book, Legacy Minded Men, resonates with me personally and what I know about the Bible. From the New International Version (NIV), Acts 13:22 says, *"After removing Saul, he made David their king. He testified concerning him: 'I have found David son of Jesse a man after my own heart; he will do everything I want him to do."* Many who have studied and read, know that David was a great sinner. He even committed adultery and murdered the man whose wife with whom he committed the adultery. However, with all of his faults...God loved David; because he a had a repentant heart. He had a yearning to please, praise, and obey the Lord and Savior and was called "A man after God's own heart."

Let me encourage you to read *Legacy Minded Men*. Take time to reflect on the circumstances and sentiments presented about men and their legacies and how you may incorporate positive changes into your life. Never forget that continuous improvement of our mental, emotional and spiritual life is an ongoing process. Therefore, read the reflections in the book.

Dog-ear pages and highlight areas that resonate with challenge you might face. It will serve as a blessing to your life's journey!

Clairmont J. Barnes, Jr
Springfield, VA
Just for Men prayer call group
Emmanuel Worship Center

DEDICATION

To the *Just for Men*, prayer call team, of the Emmanuel Worship Center, in Alexandria, Virginia. I am happy for what God is doing with the men through prayer in my ministry here, and it is my desire that the men will construct a model of ministry for multiple men around the world. The goal is to keep up the prayer attack for other men and encourage them to take time to protect their legacy in prayer.

ACKNOWLEDGEMENTS

Thanks to *Local Talk*, the local newspaper in Orange and Newark, New Jersey, whose editor and publisher requested me since 2009 to start writing a weekly opinion piece called *From the Pastor's Heart.* I began to share some pieces, directed to men, with the *Just for Men*, prayer ministry of my congregation and they liked what they were reading and suggested that I collect them and share them as a book. Thanks, especially, to brother Clairmont Barnes who offered to format and prepare this collection. It is my desire that all who read them will be find them challenging and encouraging.

TABLE OF CONTENTS

INTRODUCTION

The compilation is taken from my 2017 contributions that were published in the Local Talk Newspaper in the Oranges and Newark areas of New Jersey. I have been writing for the paper since 2009, and each year produce some 52 contributions. In 2017 the focus of the reflections was directed to the legacy of men. But, it is of interest how many women have sent messages to me that they appreciate what I have written, so I encourage that women like men can benefit from what is written herein.

While women are asking, why is it so difficult to understand the hearts of men? Men are asking the same question to women. And men are asking the same question of themselves, "Why is it so difficult to understand our own hearts"? All human beings struggle with the same issue. Nothing else is more frustrating than the failure to understand who we are. We wish to know our true feelings and our motivations, and sometimes find them so difficult. At the same time, we judge the actions of others and declare that we know their hearts. But, as is well known, "The heart is devious, who can know it?" (Jeremiah 17: 9). It is beyond all human wisdom

With such a prospect, what shall we do? Shall we not enquire into the hearts of men? My reflections suggest that we cannot allow our frustrations to stop our enquiry, for in order to have effective legacies we need to understand the hearts of men. The present compilation is an attempt at evaluation. It is not intended that we jump to conclusions, imagine strange things about ourselves or others, or make uncritical judgments, for we are warned, ""Do not judge, or you too will be judged. For in the same way you judge others, you will be judged, and with the measure you use, it will be measured to you." (Matthew 7:1, 2 NIV).

I sometimes describe the reflections as "sociopolitical discourse," because they were often inspired by what was taking place in the public arena. There I heard the perpetual debate that "even though a person is saying awful things about others" or doing bad things to others, we are to give such a person a pass, because such a person has a noble indentation and a good heart." Thus in concluding, each reflection turns to ask how God judges my heart and the contribution I am making to the future generation. What legacy or legacies am I leaving behind?

LEGACY MINDED MEN

> A good man leaves an inheritance to his children's children, but the sinner's wealth is laid up for the righteous. (Proverbs 13:22 ESV)

I remember having to learn the whole of Henry Wadsworth Longfellow's "A Psalm of Life" poem when I was in later elementary. That was very long ago. In those days, teachers would whip the students if they did not learn their poetry within a few days. Sometimes I would forget the assignment and would try to cram as much as I could, and would stand in a position in the line with three other fellow students so that the teacher would not call on us first. By the time the teacher came to us we would be able to recite the poem with a little prompting from each other, that the teacher would not notice. Of course, in other matters we were at the head of the class, so if we missed a word, the teacher would seem to give us a pass. I just wish I had paid more attention to all the poems as I should have learned them, for as I grew up I began to get the sense of what legacy we would have carried from the poets and the teachers.

In fact, I really like the lesson that Henry Wadsworth Longfellow was trying to teach us in his "A Psalm of Life." His thoughts on death in the Psalm differs from mine, to some degree. But I agree that upon death every man leaves a legacy, so we need to make sure that we do what is honorable. The last three stanzas of the poem say:

Lives of great men all remind us
We can make our lives sublime,
And, departing, leave behind us
Footprints on the sands of time;

Footprints, that perhaps another,
Sailing o'er life's solemn main,
A forlorn and shipwrecked brother,
Seeing, shall take heart again.

Let us, then, be up and doing,
With a heart for any fate;
Still achieving, still pursuing,
Learn to labor and to wait.

The message is clear that while we live we are to do all we can to leave the best legacy of life behind. The old biblical sage, Job states, that in death a person's "sons come to honor, and he *does not know it; they are brought low, and he does not perceive it." (Job 14:21 NKJV).* The wise man Solomon speaks similarly, "For the living know that they will die; But the dead know nothing, And they have no more reward, For the memory of them is forgotten. Also their love, their hatred, and their envy have now perished; Nevermore will they have a share in anything done under the sun." (Ecclesiastes 9:5, 6 NKJV).

In effect, before death comes, think of your legacy. If you wish to leave a positive legacy to those behind you, be intentional. It is not a game of chance; it is a game of choice. Choose to initiate it and direct it. Only thus can we say we are among the legacy minded men.

CAN YOU TRUST YOURSELF?

The integrity of the upright will guide them,
But the perversity of the unfaithful will destroy them. (Proverbs 11:3 NKJV)

Can you trust yourself? Should you be trusted? In our culture of suspicion these are crucial questions. In fact, in reflecting on the ongoing accusations concerning sexual harassment, being reported in the public media, this is a question that every man must ask himself? Do I trust myself? Can I be trusted? Let me leave the latter question for a future reflection and deal with the first question, "Do I trust myself?" This, in my view, should be the primary question?

A misreading and misapplication of some Scriptures can give one the impression that to trust oneself naturally leads in the wrong direction. One Scriptural text says, "The heart is deceitful above all *things*, and desperately wicked; who can know it?" (Jeremiah 19:9 NKJV). Another says, "Therefore let him who thinks he stands take heed lest he fall." (1 Corinthians 10: 12 NKJV). What does it mean, that we are never to trust ourselves? Is self-trust, all that negative? Can others trust us if we do not trust ourselves? Can God trust us, if we are unwilling to trust ourselves? Can we maintain relationships if we are unwilling to trust ourselves? Can we be left to fulfill a task without self-trust?

It seems to me clear that the answer to all of the questions raised in the immediate above, is in the negative. Stephen Covey made it clear in his 2006 book, *The Speed of Trust*, that trust is the first secret of success. He also argues that it is the key leadership competency of the new, global economy. It is most significance that we gain a positive understanding as to what is constituted by self-trust and seek to regain credibility where it has been lost, by building trust.

Here are ten fundamental strategies for building self-trust

1. Make a commitment to yourself and follow through with it
2. Make a commitment to God, understanding that only in him is victory
3. Understand that integrity is never to be negotiated
4. Understand that a good character is the foundation of trust
5. Be clear about all boundaries
6. Understand the significance of credibility – If you lose credibility you lose trust
7. Be clear about your competencies and limitations– You might not be able to do what others can do
8. Learn discern – The devil will always try to seduce you
9. Be careful; do not put yourself in conditions and situations that might lead beyond your strength. Watch who you associate with

10. Be constant in prayer, because we need strength to meet each situation

Remember that self-trust is not arrogance. Self-trust allows us to accept the reality of our own weaknesses, while arrogance will lead us to brush our weaknesses aside. Self-trust will lead us to have a sense of importance, namely that we are created in the image of God, while arrogance will lead us to blame others for any fault in our actions. Yes, self-trust does not mean that we despise others, or turn away from God. As promised, we shall speak of the latter in other reflections, but for now we conclude that much more needs to be done in our effort to build self-trust. The author of the Hebrews says, "Therefore, do not throw away your confidence, which has a great reward. For you have need of endurance, so that when you have done the will of God, you may receive what was promised. (Hebrews 10:35-36 NASB)

CAN OTHERS TRUST YOU?

> . . . Taking precaution so that no one will discredit us in our administration of this generous gift; 21 for we have regard for what is honorable, not only in the sight of the Lord, but also in the sight of men. (2 Corinthians 8:21 NASB).

I was terribly ashamed the evening when my wife and I were travelling together in our car and my cousin, who sat in the back seat, blurted out that she would not travel in a car alone with that man. We are talking about the principal of the school where she worked. She was the secretary/treasurer (as they called them in those days), and a few times we knew she went banking with the principal and on other errands. We were saying good things about the man when my cousin blurted out what was said above and more, "I would never travel alone in a car with that man. Every time we have travelled together he finds a way to let his hands pass beyond the gear lever (It was a standard shift), always seeming to make a mistake to touch my legs. At first I did not understand it, but then I came to see it was intentional." We quickly agreed with her that she needed to protect herself.

More shameful for me was the Friday night I was sitting in the church at the college where I taught. My wife was beside me, and as we watched the skit about a husband that was cheating on his wife, it displayed that the husband portended to be very religious. But as one scene concluded with his wife distraught and the children devastated, the two pews of about 14 young women, blurted out in chorus, "All men are dogs." I turned to my wife and said "Darling, did you hear that. Wow!" She tapped some on their backs and asked, "Do you have brothers?" For days I thought about the young women's perception and while I sought to minimalize the blow by saying to myself, "If all men are dogs, then I hope that none of those young women will get married to one of them, for they will be marrying one of the dogs." But I also felt the sadness of the perception, because as their professor (some of them were in my classes), I was hoping that they had seen me differently. I knew that if they were asked about me they would have no reason to categorize me thus.

Yes, the question or questions, "Can women trust me, as a man?" Can others trust me, as a person?...are questions that each person must answer for themselves! Of course, there is something vicarious by the individual answers of each man, because each woman, or each person only learns to trust others by trusting one person at a time. Just like children who have grown to trust others by first trusting their parent(s) or other caregiver(s), so trust is built, one person at a time.

One politician got it right, that having failed, he has a long way to go in order to win back people's trust. What will it take to gain the trust of others?

1. We must show respect to them
2. We must practice uncompromising love toward them
3. We must observe the necessary boundaries that make for dignified relationships
4. We must practice fidelity
5. We must be persons of high integrity
6. We must communicate transparently
7. We must always seek to do the right thing
8. We must be honest – tell the truth
9. We must be reliable – Consistency pays
10. We must show people that you care about them, not just about you and your needs
11. We must say what you mean and mean what you say
12. We must show that you can be trusted
13. We must learn when to say NO
14. We must value our relationships for the long term
15. We must live in an exemplary way

In writing to the young pastor, Timothy, the Apostle Paul offered the advice that should become a mantra for every man today, "Don't let anyone look down on you because you are young. Instead, set an example for the believers through your speech, behavior, love, faith, and by being sexually pure" (1 Timothy 4:12 CEB).

CAN GOD TRUST YOU?

> Having a good conscience, that when they defame you as evildoers, those who revile your good conduct in Christ may be ashamed. (1 Peter 3:16 NKJV).

Let us follow up from the questions that I raised in two previous reflections, namely, "Can you trust yourself?" and "Can others trust you?" The follow up question is, "Can God trust you?" This is the biggest question of all the questions, because whereas we might deceive ourselves and other people, we cannot deceive God. It has been said, "You can fool some of the people some of the times, but you cannot fool all of the people all the time." Moreover, "You can fool yourself, but you cannot fool God."

It is of interest that there are those who think they can "fool God." They say, "God does not see us" or "God does not hear us," "God is like our idols, he is blind. He is deaf. He is dumb. So, we can do as we please." To such persons the Psalmist offers the reminder, do not say, that God cannot see, hear, speak. Such is the state of the idols you worship, not God (Cf. Psalms 94:7; 10:11). In other scriptural texts it is made clear that God knows everything, he knows the past, present and future. He sees everything, all our flaws, faults, failures and our offenses. He knows our hearts. He knows out minds. He knows where we were born. He knows our works. There is nothing hidden from him. All is perfectly revealed to him. "The Lord is constantly watching everyone, and he gives strength to those who faithfully obey him." (2 Chronicles 16:9 CEV). "Nothing is hidden from God! He sees through everything, and we will have to tell him the truth." (Hebrews 4:13 CEV).

So, in answer to the question "Can God trust you?" God has spoken for himself. Here is what he said of Abraham, "Abraham will surely become a great and powerful nation, and all nations on earth will be blessed through him. For I have chosen him, so that he will direct his children and his household after him to keep the way of the Lord by doing what is right and just, so that the Lord will bring about for Abraham what he has promised him."(Genesis 18:18-19 NIV). In the dialogue of Job when Satan sought to challenge the justice of God, God said to Satan, "From where do you come?" So Satan answered the Lord and said, "From going to and fro on the earth, and from walking back and forth on it." Then the Lord said to Satan, "Have you considered My servant Job, that there is none like him on the earth, a blameless and upright man, one who fears God and shuns evil?" (Job 1:7-8 NKJV).

Wow! What a God? He trusts people, even when he knows their weaknesses. He tells us who to trust, "Do not put your trust in princes, Nor in a son of man, in whom there is no help. His spirit departs, he returns to his earth; in that very day his plans perish." (Psalm 146:3-5 NKJV). But he invites us to trust him, and he has people, even princes, that he trusts. Imagine that he entrusted the leadership of Israel to Saul, and David, and Solomon, and to the young Josiah and Joash.

Here are ten reasons that form the basis of his trust

1. He can see us through and through
2. He knows what is in our hearts
3. He not only knows our actions, but our intent
4. He knows those who trusts him completely
5. He knows the mutual nature of trust
6. He knows who are fully surrendered to him
7. He knows those who are living a life of holiness
8. He knows the way in which we become trustworthy
9. He knows that by trusting he will know what blessings to share with us
10. He knows that to love us is to open the way to our trust

Finding out whether God can trust other people is quite significant, but most significant is whether God can trust me. Can God trust me?

LIVING IN A CULTURE OF LYING

> Lying lips are an abomination to the Lord,
> But those who deal truthfully are His delight. (Proverbs 12:22 NKJV)

We condemn lying, but it is of interest how much our culture seems to be affirming it. Lots of money is being made in the movie and novel industry because of celebratory works such as "Sex, Money and Lies," "Sex, Power, Money and Lies," Sex, Texts and Lies," "The Biggest Lie," "The Greatest Lie," and other titles of the sort. They sell well. People like to look at them and read them, for they seem to say something significant about the human heart.

In the realm of politics today we are hearing and seeing it more and more. We are being inundated with lies. It is even being said that the current president of the United States lies all the time. He tells up to 16 lies per day. I do not know this as a fact. It might be "fake news." But what I know is that lying seems to be becoming quite acceptable today.

From self-deception, through marital and familial lying, public lying seems to be on the rise. What Diplomat, Niccoli Machiavelli promoted in the Prince for the retention of power seems to be becoming more and more acceptable in our public square today. At one-time honesty was considered to be one of the highest virtues for effective relationships, especially for any public rulers, at least that is what king Solomon thought of it (cf Proverbs 17:7). Today it seems we have turned away from interest in truth and honesty. We like to investigate and to name others as liars, if what they purport does not line up with our views, but are we really interested in truth?

May God help us. If we do not get out of this culture of lying, we are going to destroy ourselves. Lying leads to murder and other forms of violence. Ask David what happened after he committed adultery with Bathsheba, and sought to lie about it, how he murdered her husband Uriah? Ask Judas, how after he sold Jesus for thirty pieces of silver and continued to lie, how he offered that "kiss" that blistered on Jesus that led to the crucifixion and death. Ask King Henry VIII, how he used to lie to get rid of the wives he did not want to retain.

Lying is ruthless. Lying is worthless. Lying is wicked. Any person that depends on lying will soon destruct. Although lying has been at the foundation of our human history, as is noted from Genesis 3:4 where the serpent was in dialogue with Eve when it said, "You shall not certainly die," yet lying is not good. This is why one of the Ten Commandments says, "You shall not lie." (Exodus 20:16). Solomon spells it out this way:

> There are six things that the LORD strongly dislikes, seven that are an abomination to him: haughty eyes, a lying tongue, and hands that shed innocent blood, a heart

> that devises wicked plans, feet that make haste to run to evil, a false witness who breathes out lies, and one who sows discord among brothers. (Proverbs 6:16-19).

The point is that we cannot live in a constant culture of lies. We need a fundamental shift in our culture. We need to be more conscious about truth. We might not have our noses growing like that wooden puppet Pinocchio every time we tell a lie, but remember that we are corrupting our hearts, minds, character and spirits. All of us, who are awakening in conscience, who sense the polluting nature of lies on our personal lives and public culture, need to pray a prayer like that of David in Psalm 51. I cannot quote it all here, but in verse 10 it says, "Create in me a clean heart and renew a right spirit within me." If we cannot be transformed from the culture of lying, God help us.

A PASSIONATE SPIRIT

> Brothers, my heart's desire and prayer to God for them is that they may be saved. (Romans 10:1 ESV).

Most often when we hear the word "passion," we tend to conjure negative connotations of an angry man or a person who is overly sexually expressive. But passion is a significant gift that, as human beings, we receive from God. Someone calls it, "Our God-given capacity to attach ourselves emotionally to something or someone over an extended period of time to meet a need." Tom Peters who wrote the best seller, *A Passion for Excellence*, quite a few years back, made clear that passion is what distinguishes an effective leader from an ineffective one. For Peters, successful organizations maintain their creative and competitive edge when they are led by passionate people and have workers who are passionate.

The above leads me to ask the following questions. Are you one of those complacent souls who says what is found in the book of Proverbs, "A lion is outside, I shall be slain in the streets" (Proverbs 22:13; 26:13)? Are you fearful? How do you justify your lack of action or wrong actions? Are you one of those souls who accept mediocrity? How do you use the creative, imaginative mind that God has given to you? Yes, these questions are about your passion, that is, positive passion which should lead you to transform your

- Imagination –That helps the mind to form new pictures, new ideas in the mind.
- Motivation – That stimulates us to act in powerful ways
- Focus – That keeps us on target
- Persistence – That makes us determined and dedicated
- Risk-taking – That allows us to grasp what seems possible; and what to others might seem impossible
- Accomplishment – That enables us to make sure that a task is not accepted until it is completed
- Excellence – That will not take the path to mediocrity
- Love – That will make your affection grow stronger

The apostle Paul says we are to "Love one another with brotherly affection. Outdo one another in showing honor. Do not be slothful in zeal, be fervent in spirit, serve the Lord." (Romans 12:10, 11)

Let me ask, again, "How is your passion?" Do you have a passion for God? Do you have real motivation for Godly things? Are you fervent about your faith? Are you resolute about building good relationships?

Formulate your own questions. Check on yourself. See what you truly care about.

GAINING BACK RESPECT

> Let nothing be done through selfish ambition or conceit, but in lowliness of mind let each esteem others better than himself. 4 Let each of you look out not only for his own interests, but also for the interests of others. (Philippians 2:3, 4 NKJV).

The past few weeks have brought much pain to many hearts, as they have watched the names of many of our society leaders go down in infamy. The men have not been dragged into the mud because of some effort to scandalize them, but because of their own lack of sexual responsibility and integrity. The efforts that have been made to cover up their actions, with money, power, position, and popularity, have been futile. Women are speaking out. Thanks be to God. The women are helping to raise the question, again, about what it means to be a man of integrity.

At one-time manhood meant being a protector, that is going before a woman in face of danger, allowing a woman and a child to feel safe in a man's presence, being a builder of the society, being the head of a household, providing for the family, fixing things, and in a Christian frame, being kind and loving, like Jesus loves the church (Ephesians 5:23).

Now we face the myths that manhood means brutal strength, chauvinism, demeaning other people, overpowering women, salacious talk in locker rooms or on golf courses, and the production or viewing of pornography, and so much more that is negative about men. There is great confusion as to what it means to be a man of integrity. It is thus necessary to think clearly of what is happening to manhood. After so much has been done to transform our culture from men being responsible for the protection of women. After so much has been done to confuse the gender of men. After the acceptance that it is the privilege of men to do certain things to women and get away with it. After so much has been done to remove our moral boundaries, we have come to this moment when we need to challenge ourselves again to be men of integrity.

Here is how the Apostle Paul appealed for integrity to the men of one community he nurtured, "Therefore, be imitators of God as dear children. 2 And walk in love, as Christ also has loved us and given Himself for us, an offering and a sacrifice to God for a sweet-smelling aroma. 3 But fornication and all uncleanness or covetousness, let it not even be named among you, as is fitting for saints; 4 neither filthiness, nor foolish talking, nor coarse jesting, which are not fitting, but rather giving of thanks. 5 For this you know, that no fornicator, unclean person, nor covetous man, who is an idolater, has any inheritance in the kingdom of Christ and God. 6 Let no one deceive you with empty words, for because of these things the wrath of God comes upon the sons of disobedience. 7 Therefore do not be partakers with them." (Ephesians 5:1-7 NKJV)

May God help more men to examine and reform themselves, so that together we can gain back the respect of being men of integrity!

WHEN EVERYTHING IS SHAKING

> "Yet once more I shake not only the earth, but also heaven." Now this, "Yet once more," indicates the removal of those things that are being shaken, as of things that are made, that the things which cannot be shaken may remain" (Hebrews 12:26-27 NKJV).

Have you ever lived a day when you felt like everything was going wrong, when nothing was going right, when everything seemed like they were moving out of place, not only in your personal life, but all around you? If I might confess, yesterday I felt like that when a certain public event occurred. Although my wife and I were close in the house, for a few hours, we did not speak much, but I sensed her deep, painful emotions, as I heard her groaning in her soul all evening. The event of which I speak was so epoch making that it led me to think of that text in the book of Hebrews that says, "Yet once more I shake not only the earth, but also heaven." Now this, "Yet once more," indicates the removal of those things that are being shaken, as of things that are made, that the things which cannot be shaken may remain" (Hebrews 12:26-27 NKJV).

I do not know whether you believe that such a shaking is possible in our time. But from what I am seeing, not only in the physical world, where the experiences of earthquakes and tornadoes are coming at a pace that is baffling to scientists, but in our moral, social and political systems, there seem to be a rocking of the foundations. The earth, says the Apostle Paul is "groaning," longing for the manifestation of the children of God and the unveiling of evil, such as has never been seen. (Romans 8:19-22)

If you accept the prophetic understanding of the Bible, as I do, you should have no doubt that what the prophets predicted is being fulfilled before our eyes. Long ago, Isaiah prophesied that God will one day rise up and shake the whole earth. "Behold," he says, "the Lord makes the earth empty and makes it waste, distorts its surface and scatters abroad its inhabitants. . . In the city desolation is left, and the gate is stricken with destruction. When it shall be thus in the midst of the land among the people, it shall be like the shaking of an olive tree, like the gleaning of grapes when the vintage is done (Isaiah 24:1, 11, 13 NKJV). Ezekiel, Joel, Haggai and other prophets prophesied the same. And the writer of Hebrews repeats it: "... God is going to shake everything in sight - so that He alone is revealed as the only unshakeable power!"

In effect, we are not to be surprised by the shaking that we are seeing in just about all of the systems of the world. The word of God predicted it, and we need to be ready for it. How do we prepare ourselves for a shaking of the present magnitude? Let me suggest three things:

1. Learn to pray for critical insight into what is taking place about us so that you will not say, "Peace and safety" while sudden destruction is coming on the world (1 Thessalonians 5:3)
2. Learn to be patient. The Apostle James appealed to the community which he oversaw thus, "Dear brothers and sisters, be patient as you wait for the Lord's return. Consider the farmers who patiently wait for the rains in the fall and in the spring. They eagerly look for the valuable harvest to ripen." (James 5:7 NLT)
3. Seek to stabilize your faith in God, in every way. Faith is not by chance. Ask the Lord to establish your faith. Ask him to let your faith settle in your heart. (cf. Ephesians 3:17-19).

ON BECOMING A MAN

> "When I was a child, I spoke as a child, I understood as a child, I thought as a child; but when I became a man, I put away childish things." 1 Corinthians 13:11, NKJV).

Alongside of the Bible verses that we learned when we were boys in elementary school, was the gem, "Don't lean on others, be a man! Stand on footing of your own. Be independent if you can, and cultivate a sound backbone." I cannot remember if the girls got a chance to say it, my sisters and my wife said they did, and no explanation given. Of course, I think our teachers had a particular intention of challenging us boys to be men. In those days, manhood was taught to be something profoundly desirable. It meant that you had to be strong, courageous and independent. You had to have character. You had to have brawn as well as brains.

Our Grandma who lived at our house, was very careful about our manhood too. If we would go into the kitchen or sought to do what she perceived as "girly things," she would find a way to get us out of the kitchen, in addition to saying, "Be careful that you become a mama man." She watched, continuously, to see when the first strand of hair was going to grow on our faces and while she joked about it, she seemed gratified that my brothers and I were becoming men.

We also wanted to be men, and we did some interesting things to encourage our beards to grow, some so ridiculous that they would incur much laugher if I mention them. And when our voices began to change we wanted to know whose was the deepest. Sometimes the voices would trip back and forth and we would be scared of where they were to settle down. I did ask my mother once what was happening with my voice. I was really scared that I might not be becoming a man. But I felt gratified because by the time I was 14 I was singing bass for family quartet and church choir. And people began to take notice for one pastor's wife who taught at a college asked my mother how she could recruit me to sing in her college choir. That was part of my encouragement for thinking that I was college bound. Of course, when I heard the Vienna Boys' choir I did admire their "impressive" tenor. But on learning that in order to maintain their voices at that high pitch they had to be neutered, I said I am glad I did not have to go to that college. Those boys were never ever going to be men, in my view, at least.

Yes, becoming a man was paramount to me, my brothers and other boys in my community. In fact, as soon as we could get our hands on it we knew we had to read, Dr. Harold Shryock, On Becoming a Man. It was soft talk about *"the birds and the bees,"* and our parents, who were a little bit more liberal than most of the conservative religious parents in our area would allow us to read it. We were thankful for the encouragement to read, but more than that we had our father and a number of men in our community who modeled for us what they felt it meant to be real men. If we said we were men, they expected us to be men. We were not confused with all of this transgender stuff. We only had two genders then, as least in any public discourse, "you were a man or you were a woman." 'You were a boy or you were a girl." Am I being too nostalgic or what? I was just thinking that life today has become so complex that too few men know whether they are men or women, or what. What a world? Does my old school gem about "Be a Man" still have significance? Do the words of the Apostle Paul still have meaning? "When I was a child, I spoke as a child, I understood as a child, I thought as a child; but when I became a man, I put away childish things." 1 Corinthians 13:11, NKJV).

Yes, how important is the question, today, "What does it mean to be a man?"

A FAITHFUL FATHER

"Pure and undefiled religion before God and the Father is this: to visit orphans and widows in their trouble, and to keep oneself unspotted from the world." (James 1:27 NKJV).

One of the evidences that a man is a man is when he accepts the responsibility of fatherhood. When a man abdicates such responsibility one is confused as to what to call him. He might have children, many of them; but if he does not seek to provide for his family; if he does not seek to protect, support, guide, discipline, bless, lead and be exemplary for his children and family; how can he be considered a father?

Fatherhood does not only mean to produce children. One fellow, in discussion with me, while boasting about his fathering prowess declared that he had 24 children with several women. When I asked him how did he care for them he told me that he had done all he could do for them already. Being curious as to what he had done, I pressed him further on what he did, and without hesitation he said, "I gave them life, the rest of the responsibility was up to their mothers." I was so shocked by his rather flippant answer that I was dumbfounded as to what else I could say and quickly found a way to excuse myself.

I must admit that the example above is rather extreme to most of us who live in some parts of the world. But with 72, 52, and 42 percent of single parent families - in varied parts of the United States - with the majority being headed by women, one can be assured the practice of absentee fathers is pervasive; and the notion that the task of men is to simply produce the sperm that helps to bring forth children is reprehensible. However, some surveys have been indicating that in contemporary America, many fathers are more involved than ever before with their children, both emotionally and practically. And while Moms increasingly share the responsibility for the family's income, Dads are assisting with more of the childcare and household chores. Yet, it is clear that the surveys do not focus on the largest part of the society; so many children are still without fathers that we can actually say we are living in "a fatherless society."

Does God care about the multitudes of children whose fathers have absconded? Yes, he does. In fact he names himself, "A father to the fatherless, a defender of widows, is God in his holy dwelling." (Psalm 68:5). He not only names himself a father to the fatherless, but he makes clear that he protects them and helps them in their struggles and distresses. This is why the writer of the Proverbs says, "Do not remove the ancient landmark, nor enter the fields of the fatherless; for their Redeemer is mighty; He will plead their case against you" (Proverbs 23:10, 11 NKJV).

If you have been a good father, you need to be commended. However, just attending to your own children is not good enough, because there are many fatherless children who need your care. You might not necessarily be in a position to adopt them, but you can be a surrogate, a mentor and an example to them. In fact, the appeal of the biblical prophets was not just to assure the fatherless that the Lord would be a father to them, but it was to challenge those who were good fathers to become fathers to the fatherless. This is why the Apostle James says, "Pure and undefiled religion before God and the Father is this: to visit orphans and widows in their trouble, and to keep oneself unspotted from the world." (James 1:27 NKJV).

My prayer today is that God will not only make you a more courageous man, but an even more effective father.

BEING A TRUE HOUSE – BOND

> Forbearing one another, and forgiving one another, if any man have a quarrel against any: even as Christ forgave you, so also do ye. And above all these things put on charity, which is the bond of perfectness. And let the peace of God rule in your hearts, to which also ye are called in one body; and be ye thankful. (Colossians 3:13-15 KJV).

Let me indulge a little by sharing the news that our family just had the greatest of privilege to attend our Dad's 104th birthday celebration. The grammatical guide on my computer actually wants me to say celebrations, because it sees the 104 as plural. Dad is in his right mind, and for that we are very grateful. He talks a lot of his many years of what might be said in colloquial terms, "Water under the bridge." But he also gloats a lot for his 71 years with his wife who died at 96, a few months after their anniversary. Dad constantly boasts about the fact that his wife was the greatest woman who ever lived. I am sure that as a reader you might say that is an exaggeration; and very likely it is, but it is said, "Beauty is in the eye of the beholder." For us who have watched, we know that what is significant is that Dad has been most powerful in bonding a family.

According to the dictionary one understanding of bonding typically refers to the process of attachment that develops between romantic partners, close friends, or parents and children. Although I made reference to the bonding that took place between Dad and Mom, my larger focus is on the bonding that takes place between husbands and wives, because from what I am seeing these days, only a minority of households can say that there is much bonding. It is said husband comes from the word, "house - bond." That means, one who knows how to join people and things together, fix things and secure things. A house-bond is one who knows how to share his affection and give strong support to the one he loves. In my role as a pastor, I see and hear many women sharing their pain and requesting prayers for their husbands who they expected to be there for them, supporting them and sharing their affection and trust. While I assure them that I hurt with them and will pray for them, I also share the hurt and pain for the men around them.

Many men are not good *house-bands*, not because they cannot be, but because of their lack of proper role modeling. They have had no one to teach them how to bond. Learning bonding is not a course that one takes in high school or college; it is a life course that one takes from the earliest of childhood. And where there is a lack of good role models in the home, there will be failure from the start of life. This is why each man needs to be called upon to understand his role as model husband. He needs to know that somebody is watching; somebody is taking notes. I do not just mean that God is watching. I also mean that our boys are watching.

WE ARE TRULY BROTHERS

> Be kindly affectionate to one another with brotherly love, in honor giving preference to one another; 11 not lagging in diligence, fervent in spirit, serving the Lord; (Romans 12:10, 11 NKJV).

Three of four brothers of us came together to share in the 50th wedding anniversary of a cousin we call a brother. The day prior to the celebration and two days following, before we separated to our varied countries of abode, we shared in much fellowship together. On one of the days we went to a shopping mall with our wives and while they were gone inside the stores we stood in a little circle outside and talked much on varied subjects. We talked about our growing up days, and the pranks we played on our parents. We reflected on the times when we were whipped and what we thought should have been really done. We even compared notes on whose wife likes to shop the most and how we react to them. We spoke of sports, politics, and the condition of our health. And we each gave praise to God for how much we have been blessed, and the ways in which he has taken care of our families. The time of shopping seemed to have passed quickly, and when our wives returned we went out to eat.

As we returned to our hotels, the one brother who was absent from the occasion phoned me. I gave him time to express himself, and as true brothers like to do, teased him a little and then expressed how much he was missed and assured him that we will find a near occasion for him to be with us. Frankly, we are blessed brothers. We love each other, care about each other, support each other, and show concern for each other's family. We practice a common faith, and from all I know, all are rather fervent about the faith we share. We talk about faith and family and Scripture and music all the time. In fact, while I am a trained preacher, my other brothers are preachers too, and we are always sharing our insights on scriptural passages.

By putting this reflection in the public view, I am hoping that I did not make anyone think that we have never felt tensions between us. As everyone who has shared in them might know, the relationship between siblings is fascinating; it can inspire to goodness or introduce to vice. It can also create closest allies, or create enmity. In addition, that relationship can lead to enjoyable fellowship or resentful distancing for life. My brothers and I are blessed to enjoy the finest of relationship. We have accepted that while our blood relationship means much and our family name must be maintained at a high level of respectability, there is more to us being brothers than our blood. We were grown in varied places while in our teens as we separated for school or accompanied our parents as they traveled away from the country in which we were born to pursue a better life for all. So in looking at the years of our separation, we have concluded that it is the grace of God that has sustained us.

In order to be effective in our bonding, we decided to be faithful to each other, forgive any childish pranks we played on each other, be supportive of each other, laugh much together, pray for and with each other, and do whatever is necessary to build and keep the bond at a level that can be exemplary for our sons (and daughters, of course). We have taken the scriptural word most seriously, "Do not be like Cain, who belonged to the evil one and murdered his brother. And why did he murder him? Because his own actions were evil and his brother's were righteous" - 1 John 3:12 NIV. No, we do not allow any evil to come between us. We do not take one another for granted. We have cultivated a "stick together attitude," that might make those who cannot appreciate it rather jealous. But this is who we are and how we are. We are brothers by the blood and the Spirit.

WHO IS THE HEAD OF THE HOUSE?

> But among you it will be different. Those who are the greatest among you should take the lowest rank, and the leader should be like a servant. (Luke 22:26 NLT).

My wife and I have just celebrated 48 years of marriage. If you ask me "What's the formula, I make it clear that the "mercies of the God are new every morning, great has been his faithfulness." In addition, we are clear about our rolls. We knew in theory before we were married, but found out more practically very early that quarrels about power, positions and privileges were paths to destruction, so we decided that the path forward was to be servants; Yes, servants of each other. She does not have to tell me "Take out the garbage" or do all the human (no mistake meant) things that I do around the home. I help to clean the floor, help with the washing, and even try to cook sometimes. We do not quarrel about who is the head or who is the leader. We celebrate our equality, but give difference to each other in how we understand ourselves in what God has called us to be in our leadership rolls.

Forgive me for boasting a little but I am very happy for the blessings of God on these 48 years. And I am glad that we have not had to struggle like the one couple that I was called to counsel a few years ago. As soon as I entered the house I noted the problem, a struggle over who was the head of the house.

After they offered me a seat for the counseling period, I suggested that a seat around a table would be preferable and so we did. We spoke for a while and then a most comical moment came in the conversation; the husband blurted out, "Pastor, will you tell my wife that I wear the pants around here." I really felt blindsided with the comment and pushed back a little from the table, and then I noticed that his wife was wearing a pair of pants too. Immediately I remarked, "Brother, I see that your wife is wearing pants too." At that moment, the tension was broken and we were able to discuss, the issue at hand- leadership and control.

A lot of men and women are having problems in the above areas, which is why so many families are breaking up. Many men believe that in order to show that they have authority and are leading they have to be bullies. They believe that authority and leadership mean that they need to struggle for supremacy and be autocrats.

They think it is a power and positional thing. They forget that the best of authority and leadership are seen in service. Jesus said it clearly when he responded, "But among you it will be different. Those who are the greatest among you should take the lowest rank, and the leader should be like a servant." (Luke 22:26 NLT).

Using the word from Jesus and from all our years of experience that I have shared in marriage, I encourage every man that the best way to exercise authority and show leadership is to serve. That does not mean that you are not head of the house.

Serving will require love, humility, patience, meekness and other qualities that are not appreciated by people who are not godly, but these are the qualities that make for effective headship and successful marriages. Do you want to be more effective as the head of the house? Then be a servant.

MAKING LOVE

> "He has brought me to his banquet hall,
> And his banner over me is love. (Songs of Solomon 2:4 NASB).

I love to read the Canticles, otherwise known as the Songs of Solomon. In fact, when I attend men's conferences I like to encourage the men to take some time to read and reread this book. In a time when there is so much misconception of what constitutes romantic love, it is good to take time to reflect on a document that gives a picture that can be used to critique our present notions and practices of love.

The *Songs of Solomon* is one of the most beautiful love stories that I know. It is not mixed in with all of the sensational stuff that lace contemporary love novels. It exudes passion and patience, pleasure and purity, persistence and a perspective that cannot be dragged into the hasty love making experiences that are celebrated in an immoral culture. *Songs of Solomon* is a model for practicing love.

An outline of the Songs of Solomon shows the following

- Love's imagination (and inspiration) - 1:1-11
- Love's patience - Look at the courtship - 1:12-3:5
- Love's celebration - Focus on the wedding - 3:6-11

- Love's passion - Pay attention to the honeymoon - 4:1-5:1
- Love's covenant - Watch the pledge to have a total life together - 5:2-8:14
- Love's work - Observe the demands of staying in love - 5:2-6:13
- Love's benefits -Notice the rewards of staying in love - 7:1-8:4.
- Love's education - Give attention to the lessons of staying in love - 8:5-7
- Love's divine design - Watch God's Design for a lifetime of love in marriage - 8:8-14

Do you sense the difference between what is portrayed in the overview of the book and the hasty and superficial ways in which many men engage in love making today? If love were properly practiced, there would not be so much divorce and broken hearts as we see in our culture today. In fact, the writer of the Song is right, "Many waters cannot quench love; rivers cannot wash it away. If one were to give all the wealth of his house for love, it would be utterly scorned." (Songs of Solomon 8:7 NIV) Yes, there is a difference in the powerful emotion of love that is born of God and that which is born from the mere human desire or breast: The one lasts; the other burns out. The one is eternal in the breast; the other gets lost in the least conflict or struggle. The one is endless; the other vanishes when conditions change.

When last have you taken the time to evaluate your love experience? So many things are consuming our interests today that we hardly take time to give attention to how we love. When we do not take time to admire the one we are supposed to love; we can get our eyes easily fixed on some other person. Let us love as God would have us love.

BEING A GODLY FATHER

And you, fathers, do not provoke your children to wrath, but bring them up in the training and admonition of the Lord (Ephesians 6:4 NKJV).

At a time when so much crime and terror is being done in the name of God, it is well for us to take a moment to reflect on the significance of what it means to be Godly fathers. In fact, there is great need within our social system for men who will have godly values that can influence the generations to come. There was a time when the term "godfather" as used in certain religious communities had positive significance, reflecting spiritual men who would offer themselves as surrogates and mentors to the little ones who were being dedicated to God. Today that term has lost its positive significance.

As time passed, the term "godfather" was taken out of the pure religious culture and was transmuted into a culture of corruption, crime, drug trafficking, revenge killings, deception, and secrecy, et. cetera. Yes, the term gained so much public currency that a trilogy of movies called the Godfather was made about it. From what I have researched, the films were widely regarded as among the greatest films of all time. They were based on Mario Puzeo's novel by the same name that focused on a powerful Italian-American crime family of Don Vito Corleone (Marlon Brando).

When Puzeo's youngest son, Michael (Al Pacino), reluctantly joined the Mafia, he became involved in the inevitable cycle of violence and betrayal that was at the center of the culture of the family. The point of greatest interest, for me, is that even though the culture of the family was so corrupted by crime and violence they were still willing to attend religious services and declare their Catholic faith.

Going back to the subject of Godly fathering, I am led to raise several questions. Firstly, how do we as men act before our children? Secondly, what are we portraying to them? Thirdly, how are we behaving before them who are looking to us as fathers or spiritual mentors? Fourthly, are we portraying godlike qualities or are we confusing the coming generations with inconsistent practices? And finally, is our religion or spiritual life being used as covers for evil? The Apostle James tells us that there is need for consistency in the way we practice our religion or live our spiritual lives. James expresses such as "Pure religion and undefiled before God and the Father is this, to visit the fatherless and widows in their affliction, and to keep himself unspotted from the world" (James 1:27 KJV).

Let us not forget that we are to be true in our representation of the divine, that is, God-figures-endeavoring to live consistent godly lives before those who are to come after us.

"BELIEVE ME!!!"

> Therefore, putting away lying, "*Let each one of you* speak truth with his neighbor," for we are members of one another (Ephesians 4:25 NKJV)

It is being repeated quite frequently, that when you hear someone uttering the words, "Believe me!" after a sentence, such a person is lying. Lying has become so acceptable in our culture, that the phrase, "Believe me!" does not mean that we are listening to truth. In one of his strongest comments to people who lived in a culture of liars, Jesus said, "You belong to your father, the devil, and you want to carry out your father's desires. He was a murderer from the beginning, not holding to the truth, for there is no truth in him. When he lies, he speaks his **native language**, for he is a liar and the father of lies." (John 8:44 NIV, emphasis mine).

I do not know that everyone who makes such a declaration needs to be held as suspect, but the question of who to believe is urgent, especially in this time when accusations of sexual harassment, assaults and fake news are being pushed by so many women across the world. Who do we believe? The women or the men? Shall we just trivialize the women by saying it is merely "she says, he says," or shall we take with seriousness what is being said and investigate with earnestness the truth or falsehood of those who are perpetuating such evil. Are men to be indicted on the word of the accusers? Is there a man in the land that can be trusted, no matter how he swears to be telling the truth?

Some men are even using the Bible and the garb of being Christians to cover their oaths of "Believe me!" But can they be believed? I have never searched myself so hard on how I am reacting to who and what is to be believed as I am doing these days. I am not concerned about the news in general, much of which is being identified as "fake news", but I have been led to focus on the cases of sexual harassment, where many women have been claiming to be stripped of their innocence. I have asked the Lord, in this, to take away any of my false perceptions and prejudices so that I can make fair judgment on those about me. In fact, I said to the men on my prayer team a few nights ago, "Men we need to pray more, especially in this time when men are being accused, and our sisters are revealing their hurts, that God will help us all to humble ourselves; that he will help us to lift up holy standards of morality as we have never done before." The burden on my heart for our sisters is truly heavy, to see how many have been hurt, and the questions being raised about them: "Can they be believed? I am listening to the men who are just wishing to walk away with the comment "Believe me!" I do not know what more to say to men, but to take note of the words of Jesus that came into my mind as we prayed, "Let your yes mean yes, and your no mean no. Anything more than this comes from the evil one." Matthew 5:37 (CEB). Later in the week, as my wife and I went to an anointing service for a woman that I knew was burdened, the words of the Apostle James were impressed on me, "Above all, my brothers and sisters, do not swear--not by heaven or by earth or by anything else. All you need to say is a simple "Yes" or "No." Otherwise you will be condemned." (James 5:12 NIV).

Here are four points to direct the hearts of men

1. Let your character be filled with integrity.
2. Respect the boundaries of every woman (and man)
3. Be honest in all your dealings
4. When you say, "Believe me!" make sure that yours is a word of truth.

CAUTION! DON'T UTTER EVERY THOUGHT THAT COMES TO YOUR MIND

> Let no corrupt word proceed out of your mouth, but what is good for necessary [a]edification, that it may impart grace to the hearers. (Ephesians 4:29 NKJV).

Lately, perhaps due to our contemporary political culture, I have heard a lot of warnings from the media, stating, "Not every thought that comes to our minds need to be uttered in words."

Interestingly, the appeal is being directed to men. In the olden days, it used to be thought that men were the silent ones. It was accepted that they would think before they talk. In fact, a lot of the historical cautions that used to be given for being thoughtful before speaking, were directed at women. So the Apostle Paul could say, "Let your women keep silence in the churches: for it is not permitted unto them to speak; but they are commanded to be under obedience as also saith the law." (1 Corinthians 14:34, 35 KJV). If he were living today, I wonder what he would be instructing, especially since it seems that the tide of history has changed; and now many men are just blurting out whatever comes to their minds. And it is most unfortunate that many individuals are congratulating those who seem frozen in their minds while being loose with their lips. Those who are offering the congratulations, are saying that the looseness of the lips is a sign of strength. Of course, I know that my young teenage grandchildren beg to differ. Whenever I reference certain names in their presence they say to me, "No Grandpa, we do not wish to hear those names, they talk too loose."

What is my point, from the above commentary? Words have power. With our words we can wound and with our words we can heal. With our words we can curse and with our words we can bless. With our words we can weaken and with our words we can strengthen. With our words we can discourage and with our words we can energize. With our words we can deceive and with our words we can speak truth to power. Jesus said, "For by your words you will be justified, and by your words you will be condemned." (Matthew 12:37 NKJV). The Apostle Paul concurred in these words, "So encourage each other to build each other up, just as you are already doing." (1 Thessalonians 5:11 KJV).

In reality, we do not only impact others when we express our thoughts recklessly, but we impact ourselves. So, before you speak next time, ask what impact it will have on you, as you think of how it will impact the world about you.

Have you ever analyzed your self-talk? If you say, "I am blessed, I am cursed, I am ugly, I am stupid, I am sick," how do you think you are impacted? On the contrary, if you direct these thoughts at others, how do you think they would feel? We know that many parents impact their children negatively with unthoughtful words. We also know of leaders who destroy communities because of their thoughtless words. So, if at all you wish to bless yourself and the world about you today, make sure you refrain from saying everything that comes into your mind. Be thoughtful about your words.

BEING A COMPASSIONATE MAN

> Blessed be the God and Father of our Lord Jesus Christ, the Father of mercies and God of all comfort, 4 who comforts us in all our tribulation, that we may be able to comfort those who are in any trouble, with the comfort with which we ourselves are comforted by God. (2 Corinthians 1:3, 4 NKJV).

In June of 2013, at a meeting in Australia, the Dalai Lama called for more leaders with compassion. He went on to say, "In that respect, biologically, females have more potential," for compassion. He also states, "Females have more sensitivity about others' wellbeing."

There is no question that at this time of our world's history, when we hear so much "mean talk" and see so much oppression, abuse and indifference, that our world needs leaders with compassion. On the other hand, although there are general agreements with the second suggestion of the Dalai Lama that women are biologically framed to be more compassionate than men, many scientists contest the suggestion. Many argue that compassion is natural and no gender differences have emerged across these studies. However, that doesn't mean that men and women experience or express compassion in the same way—and that's where the science gets interesting. They argue that we might just be prone to seeing compassion through a feminine lens, and so miss the ways in which men try to alleviate suffering.

Just as there is a push back on the claim of the Dalai Lama concerning his suggestion about women being biologically more prone to be more compassionate than men, we also need to push back on the scientist who are claiming that love, compassion, and kindness are "natural" to all human beings, in their varied forms of expression.

While we might affirm, to some degree, our natural tendencies to be loving, compassionate and kind, we need to take note of the contradictions, even with the smallest child where we see that selfishness, grasping, and hostility are the drivers of the passions more than love. Growing into adulthood does not necessarily make a person more compassionate. What makes the difference is the process that comes from the transformation of the heart.

The transformation of which I speak is not necessarily found in justice education. While education has profound value, I speak of the transformation called conversion in which God plants his love in our hearts by his Holy Spirit. The Apostle Paul states that the love of God is implanted in our hearts by the Holy Spirit who is given to us (cf. Romans 5:5). He further argues, "For God has not given us a spirit of fear, but of power and of love and of a sound mind." (1 Timothy 1:7).

If our hearts are transformed, we will be more compassionate leaders, compassionate men and compassionate women. We will see the sufferings of others and be more effective in giving help to them. In the Apostolic writings we find the following appeals: "Finally, all of you be of one mind, having compassion for one another; love as brothers, be tenderhearted, be courteous" (1Peter 3:8 NKJV). "Remember the prisoners as if chained with them—those who are mistreated—since you yourselves are in the body also." (Hebrews 13:3 NKJV),

We need to teach compassion, but we also need to pray for Christ to enter into our hearts. He is known as the greatest model of compassion this world has ever seen.

ARE YOU CONCERNED ABOUT PEOPLE'S BEHAVIOR?

> Therefore, you are inexcusable, O man, whoever you are who judge, for in whatever you judge another you condemn yourself; for you who judge practice the same things. 2 But we know that the judgment of God is according to truth against those who practice such things. (Romans 2:1, 2 NKJV).

I do not know how many of us have any concerns about our behavior or the behavior of others around us, because we live in a time when we are being told that "we should mind our own business." Thus "anything goes." Even what used to be called "political correctness" (PC), is being thrown through the door for "political incorrectness". Some are blaming the recklessness of behavior on leaders at the highest level, and others on the general political environment. We know the whole nurture/nature argument, for a short time ago the blame was on the genes; that is, if one is born with certain propensities one cannot help oneself. One has to live the life of a wanderlust or what have you. One just has to do what one's genes or gender or gender orientation tells one to do. I do not know for sure, but it seems likely that the popular song writer, Cole Porter (1891-1964), who composed many great pieces for the theatre, and who lived a painfully, addictive, depressive, and at times reckless life, was predicting our times, when he wrote the lyrics, “Anything Goes”, which I argue was a biographical statement. Here is a lengthy enough piece of the lyrics following:

> Times have changed
> And we've often rewound the clock
> Since the Puritans got a shock
> When they landed on Plymouth Rock.
> If today, Any shock they should try to stem
> 'Stead of landing on Plymouth Rock,
> Plymouth Rock would land on them.
>
> In olden days, a glimpse of stocking
> Was looked on as something shocking.
> But now, God knows,
> Anything goes.
>
> Good authors too who once knew better words
> Now only use four-letter words
> Writing prose.
> Anything goes.
>
> If driving fast cars you like,
> If low bars you like,
> If old hymns you like,
> If bare limbs you like,
> If Mae West you like,
> Or me undressed you like,

Why, nobody will oppose.
When ev'ry night the set that's smart in
Truding in nudist parties in Studios.
Anything goes.

Yes, times have changed and anything seems to be acceptable. But it should be clear that God remains. God is still the same and he still expects those of his creation to behave with integrity, dignity, decency, discretion, discipline, and morality. Especially should we understand the calling to right behavior if we are children of God? In writing to his pastoral charge the Apostle Peter says: "So get rid of all evil behavior. Be done with all deceit, hypocrisy, jealousy, and all unkind speech... Be careful to live properly among your unbelieving neighbors. Then even if they accuse you of doing wrong, they will see your honorable behavior, and they will give honor to God when he judges the world" (1 Peter 2: 1, 12 NLT). Remember that our behavior affects our character, spirituality and those about us. Especially should we be concerned for the generations to come.

FATHERHOOD: TELLING YOUR STORY

> I have written to you, fathers, because you have known Him who is from the beginning. (1 John 2:14 NKJV).

My father just celebrated his 104th birthday on August 11. Whenever we gather about him, Dad uses the opportunities to tell us stories of his life. He is very persistent in his effort to communicate. Some of the stories we have heard incalculable times. However, if we have picked up on a theme, it is that Dad is especially focused on his spiritual journey. He always gives God praise for the blessings on his life and on the lives of his children, grand and great grand-children. He enquires which of the grand and great grands are doing well in school and which is in love with the Lord. He also often references how his father taught him how to love the reading of Scripture, even though his father was not able to read. His father had memorized a few texts and then he would ask Dad to read one of them, and if Dad missed a word, his father would correct him, so Dad took it for granted that his father could read, but he was refusing to read because his eyes were getting dim.

Dad was only 12 years old when his father died. He recalls that their final encounter was on a Sunday afternoon when he went to the hospital to visit his father. His father was sick, unto death, but he was conscious enough to lift his hand and place it on Dad's head saying to him, "God bless you, my son. You must learn to love God, you hear me." On Wednesday when my Grandma went to visit the hospital, her husband was already dead and buried. That was how it was in those days.

Although Dad's faith would falter after his father's death for a few years, in his very early twenties, Dad gave himself to the Lord and has been very strong in practicing his faith since. His practice of the Christian traditions, as he understood them from the Bible, and his ritual practice of worship, have been fundamental to the development of faith to us as children. It seems impossible to have ten children who are all ordained church leaders, but that is what Dad has accomplished. Mom died at 96, and when Dad offers his praise to God, his next sentence is to praise Mom.

Dad is not perfect. Is it surprising, for me to say this? I do not know of a perfect father, but from this reflection it is not redundant to say that he took with seriousness, the words concerning the law that the Lord told Moses to give as instruction to the fathers and mothers in Israel, namely:

> You shall teach them diligently to your children, and shall talk of them when you sit in your house, when you walk by the way, when you lie down, and when you rise up. 8 You shall bind them as a sign on your hand, and they shall be as frontlets between your eyes. 9 You shall write them

> on the doorposts of your house and on your gates (Deuteronomy 6:7-9 NKJV).

When last have you paused with your children to tell them the stories of the leadership of the Lord in your life and family? When last have you taken time to prophesy to them concerning what God expects of them? Do not forget that the moments that you share with them the stories of your life and the intentions of God for them, you are directing them to their destiny.

DIRTY MOUTH

> Watch your words and hold your tongue; you'll save yourself a lot of grief. (Proverbs 21:23 MSG).

I was standing in a shopping mall where a father was passing with three little children. I suspected them to be his children by their resemblances and how closely they were holding on to him. But I thought of him as being a bit careless, for as he walked across the crosswalk, he was talking on his telephone. Of course, what I picked up was of profound interest to me. The slew of profanities coming out of his mouth were appalling. I shook my head as I thought of the "poor" children. Then I asked myself what is the difference between that father and the President of the United States in his reaction to the kneeling of members of the National Football League during the singing of the National Anthem at the opening of ball games. The public media has been replaying the profanities with such constancy that it is hard not to hear it.

How different it is now, from when I was a boy when many parents did not use profanities before their children. If they caught their children using profanity, they would wash out their mouths with soap and water, literally. Such never happened to me nor any of my siblings, for our parents never used profanities in private or public. At home there was a standard set and it was made clear that profanities were only used by a certain class of human beings, who were very limited in vocabulary and dignity. In some homes the parents used the profanities before their children, but they told their children that they could not use them. We saw the contradiction for as soon as the children thought they had grown up; they began to use profanities before their parents without any consequences.

My interest in this reflection is not just to criticize those who use profanities, but to challenge anyone who might be using any form of profanity, "put down" or abusive language, to change. In calling out the Pharisees for their bitter and angry words, Jesus said:

> Brood of vipers! How can you, being evil, speak good things? For out of the abundance of the heart the mouth speaks. 35 A good man out of the good treasure of his heart brings forth good things, and an evil man out of the evil treasure brings forth evil things. 36 But I say to you that for every idle word men may speak; they will give account of it in the Day of Judgment. 37 For by your words you will be justified, and by your words you will be condemned." (Matthew 12:34-37 NKJV).

In commenting on these words from Jesus, Matthew Henry says, "Men's language discovers what country they are of, likewise what manner of spirit they are of. The heart is the fountain; words are the streams. A troubled fountain, and a corrupt spring, must send forth muddy and unpleasant streams. Nothing but the salt of grace, cast into the spring, will heal the waters, season the speech, and purify the corrupt communication. An evil man has an evil treasure in his heart, and out of it brings forth evil things. Lusts and corruptions, dwelling and reigning in the heart, are an evil treasure, out of which the sinner brings forth bad words and actions, to dishonor God, and hurt others. Let us keep constant watch over ourselves, that we may speak words agreeable to the Christian character." (Matthew Henry, *Concise Commentary*).

If you are reading this reflection, I ask, please check the next time you speak. You might not speak the language of profanity, but you might speak abusive or discouraging words. Which is to say that you need to change the word bank inside of you and pledge to speak in ways that will be a blessing to all those with whom you come in contact.

HARSHNESS OR HOSPITALITY

> A soft answer turns away wrath, But a harsh word stirs up anger. 2 The tongue of the wise uses knowledge rightly but the mouth of fools pours forth foolishness. (Proverbs 15:1, 2 NKJV)

It is truly pathetic that our contemporary time is filled with so much harshness, coarseness, and rawness. And it is evident that such have become so acceptable that those who exhibit them in the public sphere are being admired for their strength. In fact, those who are pushing **xenophobia** instead of **hospitality** are seen as our authentic men.

The negative attitudes that have been built against **undocumented individuals, strangers**, and others who might be considered, **not like us**, are what the devil has been using to destroy our spirit of love and compassion in our culture. This is why I wish to encourage us to focus more on hospitality. In 2013 Benjamin Corey wrote one of the most insightful articles in Sojourners. In it, he emphasized that true biblical hospitality focuses on love for the stranger, immigrants and the enemy. He pointed to the root of the word for hospitality as taken from the Greek, *philozeno,* which means *love of stranger* versus *xenophobia*, which means *fear of the stranger*. Then he argues that not only are we being called to be hospitable to those who are closest to us, but to those we even consider our enemies.

Corey further states that we need to make a practice of going out of our way to take care of them. When we pass a stranger on the street, we need to smile and say "hello" instead of nonchalantly looking at our iPhones and pretending we didn't actually see them. When we're at the cash register and have our order messed up by the nameless employee, we are to show patience and kindness instead of impatience and harsh words. When a person in a car in front of us cuts us off, we need to pray a prayer of blessing for that person instead of flipping them off.

It is true that negative attitudes towards strangers have been a historical problem for many millennia. However, this does not suggest that it is acceptable to God, or that it benefits the concord of our world. This is why from its earliest history as a nation, God constantly reminded Israel on how to treat strangers. And I hope that we here in America are taking note of what the Lord expects of us. Here are four of the many Bible texts that bring strong reminders.

> But the seventh day is a Sabbath to the Lord your God. On it you shall not do any work, you, or your son, or your daughter, your male servant, or your female servant, or your livestock, or the sojourner who is within your gates. (Exodus 20:10 ESV)

> You shall not wrong a sojourner or oppress him, for you were sojourners in the land of Egypt. You shall not mistreat any widow or fatherless child. (Exodus 22:21,

> 22 ESV). You shall have the same rule for the sojourner and for the native, for I am the Lord your God." (Leviticus 24:22 ESV). The people of the land have practiced extortion and committed robbery. They have oppressed the poor and needy, and have extorted from the sojourner without justice. (Ezekiel 22:29 ESV).

Yes, these reminders are important if we wish to respect our neighbors and build a strong community. We must get rid of the harshness in our culture and focus more on being kind and hospitable. Love the stranger.

THE HEARTS OF MEN

> But the Lord said to Samuel, "Do not look at his appearance or at his physical stature, because I have refused him. For the *Lord does not see* as man sees; for man looks at the outward appearance, but the Lord looks at the heart." (1 Samuel 16:7 NKJV).

The cold blooded murderous action of the many men (and women) we call terrorist these days; and the many who are being charged with sexual harassment and rape, have pushed me to reflect on the hearts of men. How can men be so hard hearted to rent trucks and use them as weapons against innocent peoples, as has happened in the many incidents from London, to Paris, to Berlin, to New York City, without the awakening of their consciences? How can a man put small doses of sterilization pills into drink that is to be shared with a friend in order to blank out their memory and then rape them? How can one man buy some forty plus guns and thousands of rounds of ammunition in order to shoot people in a crowd? How can people stand in a school zone to sell drugs to youngsters? Why do political leaders lie so much? Why is it that so many men cheat on their spouses? How can any world leader spend all the money of their country to produce nuclear and other weapons while a large number of their people are starving?

The answers are singular and simple, as is stated in the Bible, "The heart is deceitful above all things, And desperately wicked; who can know it?" (Jeremiah 17:9-10 NKJV,). Mark 7:21-23 NKJV "For from within, out of the heart of men, proceed evil thoughts, adulteries, fornications, murders, 22 thefts, covetousness, wickedness, deceit, lewdness, an evil eye, blasphemy, pride, foolishness. 23 All these evil things come from within and defile a man." Matthew 24:12 NKJV "And because lawlessness will abound, the love of many will grow cold."

There are profound problems with the hearts of human beings, and without the grace of God they are growing more deceitful, cold, uncaring, unloving, covetous, selfish, lustful, uncompassionate and psychotic. This next thought sums up what I have expressed; "If we are not careful, just as a current of wind blows through an area, so the wickedness in the world will try to consume the heart."

Have you had a heart check lately? I do not mean one with EKG and ECG, but one which gives God an opportunity to do some search. David prayed, "Search me, God, and know my heart. . ." (Psalms 139:23). The prophet Jeremiah states, ""I the LORD search the heart and examine the mind, to reward each person according to their conduct, according to what their deeds deserve." (Jeremiah 17:10 NIV). Has God had a chance to do with your heart what needs to be done to remove the deception, the coldness or whatever is affecting your heart in a negative way?

We might reflect on the atrocious things that are being carried forward by the cold and dark-hearted people in the world and forget to check ourselves for lack of love, compassion, kindness and the little deceptions that are so destructive to us and others.

So, yes, I say, let us not just comment on the deeds of others, but let us get our heart checked and make sure that we are not a cold-hearted man.

HAVE YOU HAD A HEART CHECK LATELY?

> Examine yourselves as to whether you are in the faith. Test yourselves. Do you not know yourselves, that Jesus Christ is in you?—unless indeed you [a]are disqualified. (2 Corinthians 13:5 NKJV).

I hated to go to the doctor. I was in my early 30s and had overworked. I felt guilty for making such a mess of myself, even though it was for a good cause. Every time I had a planned visit to my doctor, my fears got worse, my heart would feel like it was about to jump out of my throat. Finally, on one visit the doctor, sensing my fears, said to me, "You have white coat syndrome." I said, "What's that?" and he recited, "You have white coat syndrome, and I am going to make you come to me every two weeks until you settle down." Whatever he did, it worked. After a few months my heart settled down and I soon felt better in my mind and body. Since that time, I have been trying to make sure that in as much as I work hard, I take time for exercising, resting, meditating, eating appropriately, and being calmer about how I live my life and so on. Yes, I have been doing as much as I possibly can that will help me avoid a heart attack. Hope I can, for all that I have heard, once one gets an attack, the heart is never the same, again.

I am seeking to take care of my heart, because, *the heart* is the most important organ in our bodies. The most general understanding in physiology is that the heart is a muscular organ about the size of a closed fist and functions as the body's circulatory pump. It takes in deoxygenated blood through the veins and delivers it to the lungs for oxygenation before pumping it into the various arteries, which provide oxygen and nutrients to body tissues by transporting the blood.

If a doctor says a person is brain dead, we know that is the second to the worst news that one might receive. In fact, some people will still stand around the bedside and pray for a recovery. But if a doctor says a person is heart dead, the conclusion is the person is completely dead. A few persons have awakened from what is called being "brain dead." But people do not awaken from the death of a heart. If your heart is dead, you are dead.

The Scripture states that the heart is the core of our being. This is why we are told to keep it pure (Proverbs 4:23). We are also told that a lot of evil springs from the heart (Mark 7:21-23; Jeremiah 17:9) and that we are to guard our hearts (Proverbs 4:23fp). Further, we need to cry out to God to "Create in me a clean heart." (Psalm 51:10). But even as we cry out, we need to admit that we do not truly know our hearts, only God does (Psalm 44:25). Therefore, we are to ask God to do the operation or heart transplant or transformation that is necessary to make us into persons with new hearts (Ezekiel 36:26).

In a concluding point of reflection, I note that sometimes we are most concerned about the heart as a physiological structure, but we care less about its emotional and spiritual states. We care little about whether it has the capacity for us to love God and our fellow beings. So this is why I write to appeal that we give more attention to our hearts, which they might not die. For if our hearts are dead, we will be like "dead men walking."

Remember, "The Lord does not look at things people look at. People look at the outward appearance, but the Lord looks at the heart." (1 Samuel 16:7)

SHALL I FORGIVE AGAIN?

> "Judge not, and you shall not be judged. Condemn not, and you shall not be condemned. Forgive, and you will be forgiven. (Luke 6:37 NKJV).

Do you remember the questions Peter asked Jesus? Matthew 18 records, "Then Peter came to Jesus and asked, 'Lord, how many times shall I forgive my brother or sister who sins against me? Up to seven times?'" Jesus responded, "I tell you, not seven times, but seventy-seven times." Jesus expanded his response in a parable about an unmerciful servant whose master forgave him, but who in turn, failed to forgive his fellow servant.

I have heard similar questions about husbands, wives, other family members and a host of other people as well. How many times shall I forgive my husband's infidelity? How many times shall I forgive my wife's promiscuity? How many times shall I forgive my brother, John or my sister, Judith? How many times shall I forgive, period?

We need not repeat the Jesus answer, or spend time multiplying what he meant by "the seventy times seven" which computes to 490 times; for it should be clear enough that Jesus was not calculating about forgiveness. He was saying forgiveness is a profound necessity for relationship building. Forgive others in the same way that we have been forgiven by God. Forgive in the same way that we would like to be forgiven. Forgive in the same way in which we ask (God or others) for forgiveness. From much research many experts have been able to establish, what I too have learned over the years that forgiveness brings at least these 20 blessings listed below:

1. Health to the body
2. Peace to the soul
3. Lightness to the spirit
4. Easiness in interactions
5. Freedom from anger and resentment
6. Empathy to the heart
7. Reasonableness to the mind
8. Hope to the life
9. Focus on the future
10. Confidence in outlook
11. Overcoming power
12. Growth in grace
13. Lowered stress
14. Reduction in conflict
15. Trust in interactions
16. Vulnerability
17. Forgiveness
18. Restitution of joy
19. A deep understanding of love
20. Reconciliation in relationships

If what has been stated is correct, it seems sensible that we need to make greater effort to practice forgiveness. Especially is the practice of forgiveness needful at a time when we find that our culture is slipping into so much talk of hatred and revenge. Hopefully, before we self-destruct, there will be a pause for redirection; for as is commonsensical, no family or community or nation can survive for long in a climate or culture of hatred and revenge. In effect, let us learn to forgive, for only thus will God forgive us.

INTEGRITY

> He who walks with integrity walks securely, but he who perverts his ways will become known. (Proverbs 10:9 NKJV).

I have been thinking about integrity over the last week. My wife and I were checking through the TSA line and just about the end of the line, there was someone who wanted to do a physical check on my wife's little bag, "again." Yes, I say, "again," because when my wife travels she likes to have every little essential to make sure that in any emergency she is well prepared. I am amazed about how many little bottles of "this and that" can fit into her purse. It seems as if the TSA agents always want to verify, with a physical check, the contents of her bags. On this particular trip, while the male agent was checking I sought to engage him in "a little chit chat." After sharing with him how long my wife and I are married, he said, "I really miss my wife. We were just married at the beginning of the year, and I hate to leave her so far away, in my country, but I have to be here." What interested me though was that he went on to say "I hope she is behaving herself." I laughed and said, "I hope you are behaving yourself too, just as you expect her to be faithful." When I said that, he laughed, as if to say you cannot expect me, as a man, to be faithful. Yes, I have been thinking about the double standard. "What is good for the goose is [not] good for the gander." In some cultures of the world, or maybe I should say, in most cultures of the world, what is expected of women is not expected of men.

What a tragedy, we might say, in sexual or other relational matters; women are expected to be faithful, honest, dignified, honorable, gracious, trustworthy, sincere, and loyal, while men can be unfaithful, double-crossing, adulterous, deceptive, unreliable, dishonest, pretentious, devious and undignified.

It is a good thing that God has one standard for all of humanity and that he expects integrity from all of us. In fact, we do not need to connect integrity with sexual and relational matters, only, but with the ways in which we relate to money and all the practices of our lives. So much has been written about Money, Sex and Power, that I need not say any more here. But I take note of what the Apostle Paul says to the Thessalonians:

> You know, brothers and sisters that our visit to you was not without results. 2 We had previously suffered and been treated outrageously in Philippi, as you know, but with the help of our God we dared to tell you his gospel in the face of strong opposition. 3 For the appeal we make does not spring from error or impure motives, nor are we trying to trick you. 4 On the contrary, we speak as those approved by God to be entrusted with the gospel. We are not trying to please people but God, who tests our hearts. 5 You know we never used flattery, nor did we put on a

> mask to cover up greed—God is our witness. 6 We were not looking for praise from people, not from you or anyone else, even though as apostles of Christ we could have asserted our authority.7 Instead, we were like young children among you. (1 Thessalonians 2:1-6 NIV).

The Apostle Paul was a man of integrity. As he points out, in all operations he tried to be a man of high integrity. He understood that such integrity was not only judged by other human beings, but by God. I encourage that we need to understand the same, namely to be individuals of high integrity.

KEEPING A SELF-WATCH

> I will stand my watch and set myself on the rampart, and watch to see what He will say to me, and what I will answer when I am corrected. (Habakkuk 2:1 NKJV).

At a time when the words and actions of our political and public leaders are being scrutinized as intensely as they are, when it is most obvious that the words of only a few such leaders can be trusted, I wish to turn our eyes back upon ourselves, lest anyone think of themselves too self-righteously. Not that I am seeking to pardon the negative words and actions of our political and public leaders, but as is known, it is much easier to point fingers than to correct one's own behavior. So let me remind all who might read this reflection to keep a self-watch. As the Bible reminders us:

> Keep your heart with all diligence, for out of it spring the issues of life. (Proverbs 4:23 NKJV)

> A good man out of the good treasure of his heart brings forth good; and an evil man out of the evil treasure of his heart[a] brings forth evil. For out of the abundance of the heart his mouth speaks. (Luke 6:45 NKJV).

> The heart is deceitful above all things, and desperately wicked: who can know it? (Jeremiah 17:9 KJV)

If one is to speak appropriately and act with integrity, one needs to self-watch. Or let me suggest in longer terms that one needs to take note of what is on the following list.

Seek to understand the negative tendencies of your life – We all have negative tendencies. And we must resist them, if we are going to live constructive lives.

1. Be careful of self-trust – We all need self-trust, but over trusting the self can be a pitfall.
2. Focus on your character – Don't forget that character is most often the fountain of our words and actions.
3. Guard your thoughts – They can lead you astray.
4. Watch what is deep inside – A quake often begins in the subterranean level.
5. Evaluate your emotions – They can make you go off-script.
6. Safeguard your spirit – It can lead you to heaven or hell.
7. Be intimate with God – He keeps your conscience alive.
8. Implant high values in your heart – Your values determine your words and actions.
9. Live with accountability – Have a small group of friends who can challenge you to do right.
10. Be willing to accept correction – You are not always right.
11. Be Humble and vulnerable – Pride goes before destruction.

We cannot be too careful to guard ourselves. If we will not, we will be sure to self-destruct.

LEARNING TO LISTEN

> So then, my beloved brethren, let every man be swift to hear, slow to speak, slow to wrath; 20 for the wrath of man does not produce the righteousness of God. (James 1:19, 20 NKJV)

My wife and I were reading our evening devotional from the book of Mark some time ago, and at the point of discussion, she landed me with a question. "Why is it that Jesus said that he spoke in parables, that 'Seeing they may not see and perceive, and hearing they may hear and not understand; lest they should turn, and *their* sins be forgiven them?'" (Mark 4:12). I tried to put on my theological cap and explain that Jesus was not trying to hide truth, but there are some persons so rebellious and resistant, in the rejection of truth, that after a while it makes no sense speaking to them. They have no intention of listening or hearing, so when in contact with them, using code language will deter them from wasting your time. The wise man Solomon echoes something like this, "Speak to the wise ones, those who are willing to listen to instructions; take encouragement and share in dialogue and you will enjoy a good conversation." He also reminds us that it is a waste of time to speak to a fool.

I do not know that I made any sense to my wife, with my frank assessment of what Jesus meant, but she seemed satisfied and went off to sleep. Of course, it was not the first time that she asked me about that thought. I think she did ask me the same question when we were reading Matthew and came to Chapter 13:13 which is quite similar to Mark's account. Matthew used Mark as the foundation for writing his Gospel, so Matthew expands on what Mark says with greater detail. Matthew was daily with Jesus as a disciple, so he got the chance to listen more intimately to Jesus.

Talking about whether we can listen well or not, or whether we have a problem listening, is something of interest. Sometimes, maybe too often, my wife says to me, "You are not listening." And at those times I have to catch myself and then give the due attention for as we teach in our family life education seminars, the most effective way of keeping a relationship between spouses is to learn how to listen to each other. Especially do we challenge men, because it is one of the usual complaint of women that their husbands do not listen. And it seems to be a fact that men do not always listen well.

It is not that men are not able to listen; listening is a choice one has to make. One has to learn how to shut out the noise, turn away from the distractions, give full hearted attention and then one will listen well. In fact, listening does not only demand the ears, but it also requires the eyes, the heart and the feet.

You listen with your eyes. You listen with your heart. And you listen with your feet. You've got to move. This is the only way to avoid deception and increase one's wisdom. In these days when there is so much to see and hear, when the devil is passing before our eyes his magical arts, when we are being drowned by the cacophony of noise, we need to learn how to listen so that we can know the difference between truth and error, right and wrong.

Again and again in the Bible the instruction is given, "He who has ears to hear, let him hear." (Isaiah 6:9; Mark 4:23; Matthew 11:13-14; 13:9). Revelation adds, to the "Let him hear," "What the Spirit says to the churches." (Revelation 2:7). The point is that we need to hear, give attention, consider, grasp, accept and obey what God is seeking to say to us.

Listening provides us wisdom. It is how we learn to know truth from error, right from wrong. It also makes for more effective relationships with others and with God. And it helps us avoid disaster.

LESSONS FROM THE FLOOD

> Then the Lord said to Noah, "Come into the ark, you and all your household, because I have seen that you are righteous before Me in this generation. (Genesis 7:1 NKJV).

The catastrophic flooding that had taken place in Texas, from hurricane Harvey, is said to be one of the worst for that area, in recorded history. Thousands of homes had been flooded and destroyed. More than 30 persons have been reported dead. Thousands had been rescued. People helped people. The flood has been said to be, by a few persons, a flood of "biblical" proportions. The word "biblical" might be used without deep thought, but it makes a point that this should be a reminder that the biblical record of the worldwide flood should not be treated with incredulity.

The story of the biblical flood is recorded in Genesis 6-9 and is referenced by many scholars as "Legendary History" or "Fake-like." Some even argue that the reporting is "contradictory" and only "symbolic". The summation from the Bible is simply that as the earth became populated, humanity became so morally corrupt and violent, that God instructed Noah to build an ark, in which Noah, his sons, and their wives, together with some of the male and female of all living land creatures, would be saved from the waters. Noah entered the ark in his 600th year, and on the 17th day of the 2nd month of that year "the fountains of the Great Deep burst apart and the floodgates of heaven broke open." The rain fell for 40 days and 40 nights until the highest mountains of earth were covered 15 cubits. Thus all life perished, except for Noah and those with him in the ark. After 150 days "God remembered Noah ... and the waters subsided" until the ark rested on the mountains of Ararat. On the 27th day of the 2nd month of Noah's six hundred and first year the earth became dry enough so that Noah and his family, could exit the ark. After exiting the ark, Noah built an altar and made a sacrifice, and by a rainbow God made a covenant with Noah that he would never again destroy all life by a flood.

There are persons today who argue away the biblical story of the flood, as there are persons arguing away "Global Warming." But denials do not change realities. "Sticking one's head in the sand," does not hide one's body from the elements. Reality is reality. We can talk about the truth or "fakehood" of the biblical flood until we die, the evidence is that a global catastrophic event took place and it reversed the order of creation from its primeval beauty into what we have today. Global warming is happening and is causing the disasters that we are seeing all about us. Instead of arguing we need to do what Noah did, learn our lessons and get into action for the salvation of the earth and humanity. Put in pious speech, here are some suggestions:

1. Be prepared for salvation. The boats that were used to rescue people in Houston could not help in the worldwide flood. The great oceanic liners cannot help. Get on God's boat.
2. Do not waste time in arguments – Find out what you need to do.
3. Understand that reality is not fantasy – even if we cannot explain everything about the realities we do not see, we can still believe what God declares will take place. God say's "I will destroy those who destroy the earth." (cf. Revelation 11:18).
4. Learn to obey the divine command.
5. Learn to follow proper instruction for salvation.
6. Do what is necessary to warn people who are in danger.
7. Be a person of action to help rescue the perishing.

A song we used to sing in church, as motivation for mission effort, when we were young is ringing in my mind, as I think of the rescue missions that have taken place in Texas. A stanza of it says, "Rescue the perishing, Care for the dying, Snatch them in pity from sin and the grave. Weep o're the erring ones, Lift up the falling, Tell them of Jesus the mighty to save."

RESPONDING TO LIFE CHANGES

> "For I am the Lord, I do not change; therefore you are not consumed, O sons of Jacob. (Malachi 3:1 NKJV)

Might I ask you a question, "When last have you really sat down and considered how many changes have come into your life since you were born?" It's amazing how life changes quickly vary, and in amazing ways. Dealing with the changes can be a profound challenge if you are not ready for their rapidity. In fact, everyone needs reminders from time to time as to how swift life changes; for at different ages and stages, we might tend to forget the quickness of change.

Very likely, if you are reading my reflection, you are not my age, maybe; but at my age and stage I do a lot of reflection about the multiple changes that have taken place in my life. And I have learned that if I do not embrace and manage the changes that come upon me, the changes will manage me and likely destroy me. It's interesting to watch your life unfold. And if you are not in charge, you are certain to be frustrated.

It is a tragedy that many, too many men (I say men, because I am wanting men to confront themselves, because many tend to forget themselves) just sit by and let life's changes happen to or about them. They see the changes and have not developed an action plan to manage the changes. They go from boyhood to manhood and do not sense the differences that come to them. One day, of course, they wake up and find that they are in a very different place than where they had intended to be. To such and to all men, I say, if you must manage the changes of your life I offer ten suggestions about what I consider a powerful action plan for change.

1. Stop worrying about life's changes, life will change, so seek wisdom - the wisdom of the divine.
2. Spend less time complaining about the changes, and more time planning what you can do with the changes.
3. Write yourself a little journal of changes and see what you need to change to have positive outcomes.
4. Do not allow a day to go by without accomplishing something positive.
5. Show more gratitude to those about you.
6. Don't clutter your life with people and things that are not worth the while.
7. Build positive relationships in family, church and community.
8. Take time to do something nice for others.
9. Educate yourself, talk to smart people, read more positive books, visit places where you can build your intellect.
10. Focus on your spirituality and ask yourself about your relationship with God.

The Apostle Paul tells of the greatest prospect of life's changes when he says, "Behold, I tell you a mystery: We shall not all sleep, but we shall all be changed— in a moment, in the twinkling of an eye, at the last trumpet. For the trumpet will sound, and the dead will be raised incorruptible, and we shall be changed" (1 Corinthians 15:51, 52 NKJV).

Are you ready for life's changes? Are you ready for the final change?

LIVING THE VICTORIOUS LIFE

> But thanks be to God, who gives us the victory through our Lord Jesus Christ. (1 Corinthians 15:57 NKJV).

I don't know about you, but when I achieve any victory I am very excited; and whenever I cannot overcome something I feel very frustrated. Maybe you have struggled with a bad habit as I have, like putting the top of a pen in my ear when I am in deep concentration. I do know better, but I just do it, and the other day it landed me in the doctor's office. Wax built up in my left ear, the ear started to hurt, and I tried to use swabs to remove the wax. But I only aggravated the situation. When I went to the doctor and he did what was needed to clean the ear, I made a resolution that I am going to break the bad habit. Thus far, I am living up to it.

At the beginning of each year and each day we make resolutions to be overcomers. When they are made, sometimes there are no set strategies to make them effective. We often forget that we cannot just depend on ourselves; we need an accountability partner. In the biblical frame, Jesus has offered to help us. The writer of the book of Hebrews encourages us to "throw off everything that hinders and the sin that so easily entangles, and let us run with perseverance the race marked out for us. Let us fix our eyes on Jesus, the author and perfecter of our faith, who for the joy set before him endured the cross, scorning its shame, and sat down at the right hand of the throne of God. Consider him who endured such opposition from sinful men, so that you will not grow weary and lose heart." (Hebrews 12:13). In effect, we are to:

- Be deeply committed to Him – Commitment means that our minds are made up to correct our way.
- Be courageous - Fear will drive us "nuts" and get undefeated.
- Be watchful – Distractions will destroy us.
- Be wise – We need wisdom to make the right decisions.
- Be intuitive – Sensitivity to the will of God is very important. One cannot be too naïve.
- Be persistent – It takes tireless effort to achieve anything.
- Be persevering – The kind of people who get defeated are the ones who lack determination.
- Be in control of our thoughts - Don't allow them to run wild.
- Be careful of self-dependence and self-exaltation – Pride will destroy.
- Be prayerful – Our greatest weapon in spiritual warfare is prayer.

We do not have to be defeated. With God's help, we can live victorious lives. In fact, there are bounteous blessings for overcoming. In speaking to the churches of Revelation here is what Jesus told them:

"To him who overcomes, I will give the right to eat from the tree of life, which is in the paradise of God" (Revelation2:7).

"He who overcomes will not be hurt at all by the second death" (verse 11).

"To him who overcomes, I will give some of the hidden manna. I will also give him a white stone with a new name written on it, known only to him who receives it" (verse 17).

"To him who overcomes and does my will to the end, I will give authority over the nations." He will rule them with an iron scepter; he will dash them to pieces like pottery" just as I have received authority from the Father. I will also give him the morning star"(verses 26, 28).

"He who overcomes will...be dressed in white. I will never blot out his name from the book of life, but will acknowledge his name before my Father and his angels" Revelation 3:5).

"Him who overcomes I will make a pillar in the temple of my God. Never again will he leave it. I will write on him the name of my God and the name of the city of my God, the new Jerusalem, which is coming down out of heaven

> from my God; and I will also write on him my new name" (verse 12).

May I encourage us, as men, to seek to be overcomers, because if we are not we will end up being defeated. The overcomers life is the best. It is the life that will get us readied for the kingdom of God.

LOVE ONE ANOTHER

> A new commandment I give to you, that you love one another; as I have loved you, that you also love one another. 35 By this all will know that you are My disciples, if you have love for one another." (John13:34, 35 NKJV)

When my sons and I talk on the phone, often enough, as we are parting, I will say to the one I am talking to, "Love you son," and he will say," Love you dad" and I respond "Love you too son." The feeling of felicity and the spirit of mutuality, is powerful. Wow!

How many sons and fathers exchange the pleasantries of greeting love or parting love or friendship love, or any love at all; I do not know. What I know is that many youngsters are hurting deeply, because they do not have dads with whom they can exchange some love. Their dads are too busy, working, all self-absorbed, absent, in jail, or at home physically; but absent psychologically, relationally, and spiritually. The interactions with their sons, if any, are superficial, unemotional, or never at all.

What a blessing it is when sons and fathers can share the command of Jesus Christ, "A new command I give you: Love one another. As I have loved you, so you must love one another."

(John 13:34 NIV). Anyone who knows the context of the text, will tell you that it was after the foot-washing ceremony in the Upper Room. Jesus and his disciples were sharing supper together. This meal is sometimes referred to as The Last Supper. It was just before his death and there was jealousy in the room. The disciples, that Jesus was training to represent His kingdom, were in a struggle for who would be placed in the highest position in the kingdom. They had misunderstood the nature of the kingdom, by thinking that Jesus was about to set up an earthly kingdom. When it was time to carry forward the ceremony of the foot-washing, no disciple would dare do it; so Jesus got up, girded himself with a towel and washed their feet. He even washed the feet of the one who was to betray him. After washing their feet, and telling them that they needed to learn to wash one another's feet, he gave this command, "A new command I give you: Love one another. As I have loved you, so you must love one another."

Notice the emphasis, twice in the short statement, he says, "Love one another." The words are profoundly challenging indeed. How do you love people who are jealous of you? How do you love mean people? How do you love people who do not care about you? How do you love people who disrespect you? How do love an enemy? In his sermon from the Mount, Jesus said, "But I tell you, love your enemies and pray for those who persecute you," (cf. Matthew 5:44 NIV).

In a sermon preached at Drexler Avenue Baptist Church, Dr. Martin Luther King Jr. said, "Our whole world is facing a revolution. Our nation is facing a revolution... One of the things that concerns me most is that in the midst of the revolution of the world and in the midst of the revolution of this nation, that we will discover the meaning of Jesus.'" I add here, that it is crucial that we do as he admonished, especially as he calls us to love. It is not in the natural heart to love. Some people we are called to love might not be loving and they might not love us back, but we need to love them anyway. One day some of them might wake up to find that their meanness does not pay and they will love us back. Of course, we need not hope that the consequence of their meanness will be the only means of motivation, but that the love of God will permeate their hearts.

As men we need to learn to love. I remember a book I read by Dr. Leo Buscagalia many years ago, that had for me a most memorable note - "Love is not taught, love is caught." Love and the world will learn to love you back. "It's love that makes the world go round" as suggested by a common usage.

TEST YOUR LOYALTY

> Then David took an oath again, and said, "Your father certainly knows that I have found favor in your eyes, and he has said, 'Do not let Jonathan know this, lest he be grieved.' But truly, as the Lord lives and as your soul lives, there is but a step between me and death." (1 Samuel 20:3 NKJV)

A lot is being said these days, in the public square, especially in the world of politics, on the need for loyalty. The president of the United States has been demanding it. Other political leaders seem to be confused by it. They are firing and sidelining those they consider disloyal. Corporations, local businesses, and sports authorities, are doing everything they possibly can to create it. They want people who will stick with them and consume their products, because loyalty is considered one of the highest priority values for economic and social survival.

Yes, the question of loyalty is very prominent these days, and has always been one of the most important standards used to test the strength of any personal or social relationship. It is a fact of interest however, that we cannot expect loyalty from everyone. Loyalty is a arises from trust. It is built on the stability of a system and on one's character. Many will promise loyalty, and will not give it. They will swear upon the Bible and not stand up to it.

But my question of interest on loyalty is directed to men whom I am addressing in the present series of reflections. For example, "How well are you, as a man, showing loyalty to your family, your spouse, your children, and your God?" Loyalty means that you are being faithful to others. It asks how well are you standing fast at your post of duty? You are doing what is needful to make those to whom you are obligated successful. In doing so, ask yourself the following seven questions that impact loyalty:

Trust – Can you be trusted?
Credibility – Are you believable?
Consistency – Are you decisive or indecisive?
Reliability – Can you be depended on?
Responsible – Do you complete tasks well?
Integrity – Are you honest and upright?
Assessment – Do you know whether the basis of your loyalty is correct?

How loyal are you? Even Jesus needed loyal men. He sought them among his disciples. As he was about to approach the cross, He told His disciples, "This very night you will all fall away on account of me, for it is written: "'I will strike the shepherd, and the sheep of the flock will be scattered.'" But after I have risen, I will go ahead of you into Galilee." Peter replied, "Even if all fall away on account of you, I never will." "Truly I tell you," Jesus answered, "this very night, before the rooster crows, you will disown me three times." But Peter declared, "Even if I have to die with you, I will never disown you." And all the other disciples said the same."

Jesus, did not speak further but took his disciples to the Garden of Gethsemane where they were tested, and they failed twice. At the moment when they should have prayed with him, they slept. And when soldiers came to arrest Jesus they fled. They failed on loyalty.

Again, loyalty is important, but make sure that your loyalty is for the right principle, value and person. Loyalty that fails to assess what it is all about can be quite destructive. So test your loyalty.

MAD MEN

> Like a madman who throws firebrands, arrows, and death, Is the man who deceives his neighbor, And says, "I was only joking!" (Proverbs 26:18, 19 NKJV).

Most of the mass killings that have been taking place across the United States of America, have lately been blamed on "mad men" (insanity, mental illness) instead of guns. Of course, what might one expect when a gun (or multiple guns and ammunitions) falls into the hands of individuals with mental illness? It is a tragedy that we treat mental illness so nonchalantly, at least when it is connected to gun crimes.

Think about it, in many cultures, mental Illness is treated as demon possession and guns would not be given to any so possessed. Maybe we need say, thank God, in the United States that the label of demon possession is not being used to trivialize people's mental condition. And yet, it needs to be understood that the devil is ever seeking to manipulate the minds of men, so that in their depressive and oppressive states, they will do things that are profoundly tragic. When a man beats up his wife at home, is he mentally ill? When a father abuses his children, is he mentally ill? When a man rapes or sexually abuses a woman, or a minor (boy or girl), is such a person mentally ill? When a man projects the evil of his character, and affixing derogatory names to almost everyone, is he mentally ill? Mental illness is not to be thought of only in the context of excessive abnormal acts, but might be expressed in marginally strange acts.

Of course, the point of my reflection is not to offer a diagnosis by the description of what constitutes mental illness, but to raise a question, to any one reading this reflection, namely, how are you taking care of your mind? The science of the mind has become a priority for researches today, because of the desire to understand how the mind works. I would suggest that we need to give the understanding of the mind priority, too, to help us in a time when there seems to be a demonic attack on the minds of so many. Or let me set forth twelve subsidiary questions, to follow my initial question, as to how we should be taking care of our minds?

1. How clear is your mind? Do you take time to unclutter your mind?
2. Do you understand that your health starts in your mind?
3. Do you make sure to think on positive things?
4. Do you read that which will elevate your mind?
5. Do you take time to slow down from your busyness to refresh your mind?
6. Have you learned how to monotask, so that your boast about multitasking will not confuse your mind?
7. Do you look at trashy movies and read dirty books and magazines that mess up your mind?

8. Do you use opioids and other forms of mind altering substances?
9. Do you meditate on the words of Scripture daily and allow it to calm your mind?
10. Have you learned to be thankful for the blessings of life?
11. Do you harbor resentment or forgiveness in your mind?
12. Do you seek to overcome your fears with a constancy of trust in God?

If you do not take care of your mind, you will become "a mad man," in a mild or excessive way. Madness or mental illness is a tragedy for any human being. It is a burden for any family. It is a problem for any society. Which is to say, we need to do all we can to maintain healthful minds. Let me precise what the Apostle Paul calls for in Scripture, "Let the mind (of God) be in you which was in Jesus Christ." (Philippians 2:5).

MEETING "FIRE WITH FURY"

> Therefore, "If your enemy is hungry, feed him; If he is thirsty, give him a drink; For in so doing you will heap coals of fire on his head." Do not be overcome by evil, but overcome evil with good. (Romans 12:20, 21 NKJV).

We were all amazed when the president of the United States responded to the North Korean test firing of ICBMs and blustering rhetoric with the words that say America was ready to meet "fire with fury." I do not wish to linger on the president's comment or offer a criticism of the language or even that of the North Korean leader; the public media has done all of that commentary and criticism. However, let me use the fact of the threatening actions and language to ask those of you who are reading this reflection a few questions. What has been the impact of such actions and language in the history of human life? What has revenge gained us? From all the international wars that have been fought, or all the negative actions that have taken place in our local communities, on the streets of our lands, our work places, our churches, our homes, and in every place where the spirit of revenge has been prevalent, what have we gained?

I do not think that I need to provide an answer, because we all know that revenge brings destruction to any personal life and to all the contexts of life named above. In fact, throughout the Bible we have been warned about the "eye for an eye" behavior. Jesus challenged those who were encouraging it with his reformed ethic, "You have heard that it was said, 'An eye for an eye and a tooth for a tooth.' But I tell you not to resist an evil person. But whoever slaps you on your right cheek, turn the other to him also." (Matthew 5:38, 39 NKJV). The Apostle Paul follows in the same train of thought; "Repay no one evil for evil. Have regard for good things in the sight of all men. If it is possible, as much as depends on you, live peaceably with all men. Beloved, do not avenge yourselves, but rather give place to wrath; for it is written, "Vengeance is Mine, I will repay," says the Lord." (Romans 12:17-19 NKJV).

I do not know that the words of Jesus or Paul or that of the biblical prophets and sages, who counseled concerning the attitude of revenge, will solve international problems, but it is good to pause and listen to such counsel and ask ourselves, personally, how else might we go about our relations with others, rather than living by the constant revenge. All of us, at times, might be tempted to make others feel the same pain that they have sought to dish out at us. All of us might be desirous of "taking things into our own hands" instead of leaving them to God. But we are also to be reminded that if we dig a pit, we need to dig two, or if we build a gallows, we need to build two. Haman learned a hard lesson, when he sought to destroy the Jews (Esther 3). Also, remember the words of Francis Bacon, "A man that studieth revenge keeps his own wound green."

As has been said, my focus is not to be a diplomat, but to encourage those reading this reflection to focus more on the language of love, the language of peace, and the language forgiveness, rather than the language of revenge. We cannot live by revenge. That is the point. Should we seek to do so we will destroy ourselves.

MEN AND OBEDIENCE

> "But they refused to heed, shrugged their shoulders, and stopped their ears so that they could not hear. 12 Yes, they made their hearts like flint, refusing to hear the law and the words which the Lord of hosts had sent by His Spirit through the former prophets. Thus great wrath came from the Lord of hosts. (Zacheriah 7:11, 12 NKJV).

These days, many individuals seem to be offended at the mention of the word, "obedience." Some persons are arguing that, "Obedience is oppressive." "It is old fashioned." "It limits freedom." "It restricts self-determination." "It inhibits independence." "It calls for too much conformity." The word is especially negative to some men. They say, "I'm a man - a grown man and I need to be able to do as I please." Or "a man got to do what a man got to do." Women might phrase their desires in other ways but they too are not comfortable with the word. In essence, all kinds of arguments are put forward to dispose of any talk or practice of obedience.

In the times in which we live, there seems to be the feeling that there is great contradiction between love and obedience, faith and obedience, freedom and obedience and the like. However, what I wish to state in the present reflection is that such contradictions arise when obedience and its balances are misunderstood. In the Bible we are told that when obedience, love and faith were disposed of, our first parents got into so much trouble that they were cast out of their garden home. Their disobedience brought the whole of humanity into a desperate situation called sin, and that is the state in which we find ourselves today. (Genesis 3). As Paul says, "Therefore, just as through one man sin entered the world, and death through sin, and thus death spread to all men, because all sinned." (Romans 5:12 NKJV).

In effect, obedience has it consequences as does disobedience. In recalling Israel to their covenant relationship with God, the prophet Isaiah said, "If you are willing and obedient, you will eat the good things of the land; but if you resist and rebel, you will be devoured by the sword." For the mouth of the Lord has spoken." (Isaiah 1:19-20 NIV).

What is clear from the above is that everyone can choose to obey or not to obey. From the biblical perspective, the choice is between God and human beings. When the will of human beings contradict the will of God, the choice needs to be clear, as Peter and John showed when they were being brought to trial before the Jewish Council, called the Sanhedrin. They said, "We must obey God rather than human beings." (Acts 5:29). Daniel and his friends made the same decision when they were brought into Babylon from Judah. They refused the king's food (Daniel 1). When the friends were asked to worship the golden image that king Nebuchadnezzar had set up, they chose to worship the God of heaven and were cast into a burning furnace (Daniel 3). When Daniel had to make a choice between obeying the decree that king Darius had made concerning not praying to the God of heaven for a number of days, Daniel made his choice and prayed at his window with his face turned toward Jerusalem. He was reported to the king who consented for Daniel to be cast into the lion's den. He was not hurt by the lions and the next day the king ordered that he be taken out. (Daniel 6). Jesus was obedient unto death. He gave up his place at the Father's right hand and came as the Incarnate One and "was obedient unto death, even death on a cross." (Philippians 2:5-8). Yes, all the ones I have cited and all the human beings have to make a choice.

One can choose to be obedient or one can choose to be a rebel. The primary choice that every one of us has to make is between God and any human being. Are we going to be obedient to God or obedient to humanity? When the will of humanity contradicts the will of God, who will we choose to obey? In these times when dictatorships are on the rise, who are we going to obey? Such remain the eternal questions. God said, "Obey my voice and I will be your God." (Exodus 19:5; Jeremiah 7:23).

MEN AND THEIR MOTIVES

> We justify our actions by appearances; God examines our motives. (Proverbs 21:2 NKJV)

In the ongoing reflection on the deadliest mass shooting that has taken place in modern American history, by one who is called the "lone wolf," a central question that is being raised is, "What was his motivation?" We have been hearing the question very loudly in the public media, again and again, and sense the bewilderment. Whoever does not have interest in this story must be really out of this world for 58 people are dead plus Stephen Paddock, the gunman, and 530 wounded, latest count. Great efforts have been made by multiple investigating authorities to check into Mr. Paddock's background. The list of the directions being pursued is long.

1. Was he influenced by ISIS? – Nothing is confirmed here.
2. Was he angry at being divorced? – Does divorce make a man a murderer?
3. Was he angry about his losses in Vegas? – He lost more than $10,000 in a few days. Was he hiding from the government or seeking a revenge?
4. Was he into money laundering? He sent $100,000 to the Philippines a few days before.
5. Was he unstable? - He lived in several places.

6. Was he crazy? He has been called "a crazed lunatic", by quite a few.
7. Was it "like father like son"? His father was a criminal, who robbed a bank and spent many years in jail.
8. Did he write out a plan for the crime? He drove 80 miles from his home in Mesquite to Las Vegas and spent 3 days in a hotel room from which he committed the crime. Checks have been made everywhere and no one can find a trace of any "derogatory" information.
9. Was he simply addicted to guns and the addiction over-powered him? The authorities found 23 guns in the hotel room, 19 at his home in Mesquite, Nevada and 5 in another home in California. About 47 guns, thus far.

These and many other areas have been checked to determine Mr. Paddock's motivation(s). It is said that until now nothing has been found. So the conclusion, is that no one might ever identify his motivation(s)?

Of course, I have a suggestion that I shall put in the form of a question. Has anyone ever heard of the biblical diagnosis on the heart of human beings? The prophet Jeremiah tells, "The heart is deceitful above all things, and desperately sick; who can understand it?" (Jeremiah 17:9). Has anyone ever heard of "Demon possession?" Has anyone ever heard of sin in the souls of human beings and in society? The great American Psychiatrist, Karl Menninger ask the question in one of his books thus, "Whatever became of sin?" In the rest of the book he went on to state that "Sin has become almost a non-entity – even in some church circles." Do we take the question of sin in the heart seriously enough? Do we think we can put guns into human hands and the demons of sin will not rise up, and cause them to be used to kill masses? I have read somewhere that when Christ came the first time, "the very stamp of demons was upon the faces of men." "The organs of men were being worked by demons." Sounds crass? But are we not facing such a time again? Are we not seeing demonized human beings enough to know motivations for evil?

We might not know each person's proclivity to do a particular act of evil, but there is no question that there are problems with the hearts of men. We are told by the prophet Jeremiah, "I the Lord search the heart and test the mind, to give every man according to his ways, according to the fruit of his deeds." (Jeremiah 17:10).

Watch your motivations? Check your heart? Evaluate your thoughts.

MEN IN BONDAGE OR FREED MEN

> For you were called to freedom, brothers. Only do not use your freedom as an opportunity for the flesh, but through love serve one another. Galatians 5:13 ESV).

As I was thinking about the issue of men in bondage, I decided to do a bit of research on the internet, on the topic. The first thing that caught my attention was a blog of some "Seabondagesadist" men. That is, men who chain, rope and lock themselves in painful, immovable positions to be taught submission. As you will see the composite word "Seabondagesadist" has in it "sadist," that tells that these men are subjecting themselves or being subjected to the cruelest of treatments. I questioned why they treat themselves thus, and do not have all the answers, but one thing I am sure of is that while their bodies are being thus brutalized by the shackles, their minds and wills are being surrendered to forces of evil that are certain to destroy them.

And while I was thinking of the men who are willing to subjugate themselves into captivity, as we have described above, I was also thinking of the multitude of men (and women) in our world today, who are giving their hearts and minds and wills over to forces of evil that are marching them into destruction. Their bondage might be some form of drugs or sexual addiction, or some materialist connection, or it might be some demonic ideology; the forms are multiple. What concerns me is that if they cannot be freed they are bound to self-destruct.

Yes, "God has called us," as human beings, "to freedom." We were created free beings, but too many have given themselves over to be subjected to forces of evil from which they cannot extricate themselves. Of course, there is a way of escape. Stated in the words of the Apostle Paul to the Galatians, "For you, my brothers, were called to freedom; only do not let your freedom become an opportunity for the sinful nature (worldliness, selfishness), but through love serve and seek the best for one another." (Galatians 5:13 AMP). The Apostle Peter says it too, "Live as free people, but do not use your freedom as a cover-up for evil; live as God's slaves." (1 Peter 2:16).

What powerful appeals. Let us not forget them. We have been given freedom. Our minds, hearts and wills are given to control us. They regulate our desires, they teach us what to choose, and how to choose. They guide our determinations.

God has given us freedom, and God does not control what we choose or the way we choose. It is up to us to choose. We can choose what is right or wrong, good or evil and what is righteous or sinful.

The simple appeal, from the reflection, is that we need to choose the right. In effect, do not bind yourselves in ways that your freedom is lost. Our world has enough enslaved men, and you or I should not choose to be one of them.

MEN OF CHARACTER

As in water face reflects face, So a man's heart reveals the man (Proverbs 27:19 NKJV)

Having watched the disgraceful downfall of some of the world's most influential men over the years, my attention is drawn to a theme that, for three centuries, had formed the foundation of culture, namely, character. Even when I was in elementary, high school and college, in the latter part of the last century, emphasis was still given to the theme, character. We were taught the significance of growing up to be "men" of character. We were told, by our teachers and parents that "the strength of a man is his character." We had to read books, and memorize poems, that emphasized the significance of **character**. At home and church our Bible curriculum called for **character** development.

Today, it seems, that character has been replaced by personality. It seems evident, that many who had been trained to regard the high value of character have cast aside such interest. In the search for today's leaders both in the public and private spheres, what is being sought is personality rather than character.

Personality, as we know, focuses on the external. It pays greatest attention to reputation, wealth, charisma, charm, dress, accent, or to such things as power, position, possession, and popularity.

Personality is about the self, the ego. And for all we know, the ego is fragile and can easily be destroyed. It is easy to be deceived by personality. So we need to be careful about giving too much emphasis to personality.

Character, on the other hand, is focused on what is at the heart of one's being. It is what transforms one's ego, because it gives attention to morality, values, principles, virtues, commitments and consistency. Character is **the mark** on the soul. It is said:

1. You cannot pay someone to develop your character. One has to work on one's own character.
2. You do not develop a character overnight. You cannot "cram" for character development. It takes time, a life time.
3. You have to be disciplined to develop a good character. It is like developing your muscles. You have to engage, consistently, in rigorous exercise to build up and maintain character development.

What the Apostle Peter said to the Christians in Rome has great relevance for the understanding of character development, namely:

> For this very reason, make every effort to add to your faith goodness; and to goodness, knowledge; 6 and to knowledge, self-control; and to self-control, perseverance; and to perseverance, godliness; 7 and to

> godliness, mutual affection; and to mutual affection, love. 8 For if you possess these qualities in increasing measure, they will keep you from being ineffective and unproductive in your knowledge of our Lord Jesus Christ. (1 Peter 1:5-8 NIV).

How significant are the steps that Peter lays out for the development of character? Should we care about character in our world of today? When we long for men or women to lead, should it matter whether they are people of character? For all that is evident to me, the world desperately needs men of character.

MEN OF POWER

> So he said to me, "This is the word of the LORD to Zerubbabel: 'Not by might nor by power, but by my Spirit,' says the LORD Almighty. (Zechariah 4:6 NIV).

A lot of books have been written over the years titled *Men of Power*. Each book has carried its own point of view, such as focusing on men of power in trade unions, the army, in public and political spheres, those who have wealth and those who have been dominant in sports. Within our contemporary culture it seems that the prevailing emphasis for finding who the powerful men are has directed the focus to those in politics, those who have wealth, and successful sports persons. These individuals are often spoken of with reverence, in many instances. Some among these men tend to speak arrogantly, with almost a total disregard for the feelings of those they think below them. However, at the same time, they call for the admiration of other men. Those who are most popular think it is their privilege to use their capacity to control other men.

In giving serious thought to the above, I have pushed myself to ask several questions, some of which are listed below.

1. What of their integrity?
2. What of their respect for other men (and women)?
3. What of their personal discipline?

4. What of their dignity?
5. What of their morality?
6. What of their love and compassion?
7. What of their sense of justice?
8. What of their care for family?
9. What of their truthfulness in service?
10. What of their honesty, before God and humanity?
11. What of their relationship with God?

Did you ever think that the world's conception of "men of power" could include such men like Adolf Hitler, Saddam Hussein, Benito Mussolini, Maximilien de Robespierre, Rasputin, Idi Amin, Pol Pot and other such evil characters? How do you measure them?

My reason for presenting this reflection is to ask, "Who comes to your mind when you think of "men of power"? Or when you think of yourself as a possible man of power, what are you thinking? Let me encourage that you give attention to what the Lord says through the prophet Zechariah to the great leader Zerubbabel who was called to rebuild the Jerusalem temple after its many years in the dust.

> "This is the word of the Lord to Zerubbabel:
> 'Not by might nor by power, but by My Spirit,'
> Says the Lord of hosts. (Zechariah 4:6 NKJV)

Yes, to be a man of power is to be imbued with the Spirit of God. You might already know, and I trust you do, that when the Spirit comes into us, or upon us, we are transformed from the weak contradictions within our frame to being powerful men. Our hearts, thoughts, attitudes are regenerated so that we can answer affirmatively to the questions listed above. In effect, to be men of power means being men of the Spirit.

MEN UNDER INVESTIGATION

> I, the Lord, search the heart, I test the mind, I test the mind, Even to give every man according to his ways, According to the fruit of his doings. (Jeremiah 17:10 NKJV).

One of the most popular phrases we hear these days is "men under investigation." Whether it is for sexual assault, homicide, drug trafficking, police shootings, arson, Russia's interference in the 2016 American Election, or the firing of the FBI Director, the news media is filled with stories of people under investigation. This leads me to ask, "Suppose you were under investigation, what would be found about you?

Quite a few years ago, the question came to mind, but developed an urgency when President Clinton was being investigated for his dealing with Monica Lewinsky. I hope I remember it right, but the sum of $750,000 which was spent for the copier used for the documents, startled me. In addition, other costs connected with the investigation were enormous. In view of the intensity of that investigation, I have often asked, what if they were investigating me? Would they find me clean? Would I be exculpated? Would I be incriminated? Then my mind projected to the biblical story of Daniel. If you do not remember the story, let me quote a little piece from Daniel 6:1-5 (NKJV):

> It pleased Darius to set over the kingdom one hundred and twenty satraps, to be over the whole kingdom; 2 and over these, three governors, of whom Daniel was one, that the satraps might give account to them, so that the king would suffer no loss. 3 Then this Daniel distinguished himself above the governors and satraps, because an excellent spirit was in him; and the king gave thought to setting him over the whole realm. 4 So the governors and satraps sought to find some charge against Daniel concerning the kingdom; but they could find no charge or fault, because he was faithful; nor was there any error or fault found in him. 5 Then these men said, "We shall not find any charge against this Daniel unless we find it against him concerning the law of his God."

The rest of the story is that all the satraps (governmental leaders) went to King Darius, with a plot that no one should offer any petition to any god or person, other than the king, for thirty days. They got the king, unknowingly, to agree to their plot and made it a statute, with the declaration that whoever disobeys would be thrown into the lions' den. Having secured their devious plot, they launched their investigation to see what Daniel would do. Without giving them the least attention, Daniel continued his usual routine of praying to his God, three times per day, with his face turned toward the city of Jerusalem. The satraps seized the moment and quickly reported Daniel to the king. The king sadly, had to uphold the statute he had unwittingly signed and had Daniel cast into the lion's den.

The story is profoundly interesting. You can read it again, as it shows how God overruled the resentment and vengefulness of the men and the pride of the king to save the life of Daniel. Of course, what lingers in my mind from Daniel's experience is the question raised above, "Suppose they should launch an investigation against me, what would they find?" My hope is that the charge would be that they would find me a praying man, praying to God and God alone. I am challenged daily, as to how I live my life. Is it a life of integrity? How is my character? How principled are my actions? Am I like Daniel or like some being investigated in our contemporary culture who are piling lies upon lies until they are caught?

Maybe we are not to worry so much about humanity investigating us, for there is a larger investigation going on in the divine judgment. As the Apostle Paul says: "For we must all appear before the judgment seat of Christ, that each one may receive the things done in the body, according to what he has done, whether good or bad." 1 Corinthians 5:10 NKJV).

THE CONSCIENCES OF MEN

> Let us draw near with a true heart in full assurance of faith, having our hearts sprinkled from an evil conscience and our bodies washed with pure water. (Hebrews 10:22 NKJV).

Sometime ago, I was reading a book that sought to make a case against the usual tests that are used to know whether or not people are liars. On the one hand, some people giggle, while others do superfluous strange things, even when they are telling the truth. Their responses might depend on how much pressure they are under, and the type of personalities that they are. On the other hand, some persons who are consummate, unrepentant liars can keep a straight face, and are so good at controlling their public persona that their biggest lies often pass for truth. In fact, it is argued that people in prominent positions who lie are often given the benefit of the doubt, and are not judged as harshly when they lie. Even those who test them are sometimes prejudiced toward them.

In effect, some people's consciences are dead. Their consciences are "cauterized" or as is said in the colloquial frame, they are **toasted**. They have no **ethical, spiritual, moral or social compasses that distinguish right from wrong**. If someone should ask, how can people perpetrate and perpetuate genocidal crimes, terrorism, serial murders, serial rape, incest, and molestations? How can people use their elected positions to lie and abuse others without any trepidation of conscience? How can people steal from church without feeling guilty? How can a man or a woman cheat on their spouse, without any sense of guilt? There is only one answer, "A seared or bronzed conscience."

In speaking with reference to the Great Apostasy of the Last days, the Apostle Paul says, "Now the Spirit expressly says that in latter times some will depart from the faith, giving heed to deceiving spirits and doctrines of demons, 2 speaking lies in hypocrisy, **having their own conscience seared with a hot iron**, 3 forbidding to marry, and commanding to abstain from foods which God created to be received with thanksgiving by those who believe and know the truth" (1 Timothy 4:1-4 NKJV).

What is of interest is that the conscience does not become "seared "or "bronzed" in a day or overnight. It takes time. Little by little a person begins to push the boundaries. Little by little the child predator watches a child, and then the first violation and a second and a third, until the person becomes a predator. Day by day, week by week, or month by month, the conscience is slighted and what used to be forbidden becomes acceptable, what used to be condemned, becomes normal. The conscience soon forgets the debate. It stops feeling conscious. It stops asking questions. It loses the quickness of sensitivity, and very soon it settles. It gets comfortable with that which formally brought hurt. It no more gets wounded. It no more feels regrets. In fact, Lady McBeth's conscience was in a better place than that of many men.

The seared conscience goes on its way without feeling. That which was added to it by God, to make it come alive is driven away. Thus the conscience fails to criticize itself, or accept the criticism of others, or even subject itself to the Holy Spirit's appeal. It dies the death of an animal without conscience.

Of course, thanks be to God that the majority of humanity are not in the state of a dead conscience. They are not totally dead, but their consciences are blunted. They do not hear, or see, or feel, or taste, with the authenticity of the divine as they used to. They break the law of God and feel very little guilt of it.

Here are five thought provoking questions to challenge your conscience

1. How sensitive is your conscience?
2. How responsive is your conscience?
3. How thoughtful is your conscience?
4. How conscious is your conscience?
5. How awake is your conscience?

Check yourself. Is your conscience dead or alive? Is it clean or unclean? We need to be serious. Let's check ourselves.

"MY WORD IS MY BOND"

> But let your 'Yes' be 'Yes,' and your 'No,' 'No.' For whatever is more than these is from the evil one. (Matthew 5:37 NKJV).
>
> "If a man makes a vow to the LORD, or takes an oath to bind himself with a binding obligation, he shall not violate his word; he shall do according to all that proceeds out of his mouth." (Numbers 30:2)

When elections are completed, I have asked how many of the promises made in the campaigns will be kept. That aside, my interest here is to ask the people who are reading this reflection, how many of us can say without equivocation "My word is my bond." Over the years I have met a lot of men who are in situations that need transformation, but when I ask them to make a promise as a way to get out of their situation, many, too many, say to me, "I won't promise." When I hear them say that I worry for them, for the fulfillment of a life purpose depends on the promise or promises such a life is willing to make to oneself and to others.

What is it that keeps people from making promises? Even though the very men that I referenced above like to deny it, I find that they are fearful - fearful of failure. Many of them are quite insecure. They lack the stamina in their will. They do not have a serious depth of conviction. And many, too many, cannot live by the truth.

But, as I have stated, it is tragic when a person cannot say, "My word is my bond," and stick by it. If one is willing to live by one's word, people will learn to trust such a person. Our society is struggling with a trust deficit, not just in the political culture, but in our families. In many cases, too many men who should set a culture of trust are too faint-hearted to make commitments and stick by them. The most respected men in the world today are those whose words can be trusted. In effect, a man who stands by his word not only gains trust but respect. And let us not forget how it also impacts the consistency of our character.

Ultimately, we are not to be only concerned about what people think of us; but what God thinks. Can our word pass the scrutiny of the divine? When we stand before God and make a promise do we live up to it? Do we seek his help to stick by what we say? The word of God tells us, "If a man makes a vow to the LORD, or takes an oath to bind himself with a binding obligation, he shall not violate his word; he shall do according to all that proceeds out of his mouth. - (Numbers 30:2).

Let us therefore resolve that we will be faithful with our word. By the grace of God, we can say, "My word is my bond."

OBSERVING BOUNDARIES IN RELATIONSHIPS

> I beseech you therefore, brethren, by the mercies of God, that you present your bodies a living sacrifice, holy, acceptable to God, *which is* your reasonable service. 2 And do not be conformed to this world, but be transformed by the renewing of your mind, that you may prove what is that good and acceptable and perfect will of God. (Romans 12:1, 2 NKJV).

Whenever I play or watch baseball, soft ball or cricket, I am very fascinated when a ball is hit beyond the boundaries. Often enough, people have the tendency to think that those who hit the ball beyond the boundaries are strong and likely, very effective players. However, in focusing on boundaries in other contexts, it is clear to me that those who like to cross boundaries are often the weakest of the weak.

In discussions with friends and acquaintances, I have become aware of a number of tragic events in which, as the reports echoed, "The men did not know their boundaries." And in reflecting on the reports I have agreed that the men needed to observe healthy boundaries.

Boundaries are important. They need to be set, known and observed. Why? Because boundaries facilitate:

1. Effective communication – Understanding communication boundaries teach us what to say, how to say what we say, when to say it, and where to say it. In the world of public media today, a lot of boundaries are being crossed, and having negative impact on the respect that we have for each other. Our children are also noticing and many are mimicking the behavior.
2. Healthy behavior – Boundaries make us accountable, not only to ourselves but to others. They help us live with honesty and integrity.
3. Self-definition – Boundaries teach us worth. They guard our identity.
4. Our choices – Boundaries define our choices. They teach us what to accept and what not to accept.
5. Protect us against destruction – Boundaries help us to know when to say YES and when to say NO.
6. Guarantee our success – Successful people know boundaries. They stay within boundaries.
7. Helps us avoid dysfunction – Boundaries help us build healthy relationships and avoid brokenness.

God has given to humanity Ten Commandments to define our life's boundaries. They are detailed in Exodus 20; Deuteronomy 5, and in varied ways all over the Bible. In shortened format, they speak of our love relationship with God and our fellow humanity. Deuteronomy 6:5 says, "Love the LORD your God with all your heart and with all your soul and with all your strength." And Leviticus 19:18 says, "Do not seek revenge or bear a grudge against anyone among your people, but love your neighbor as yourself. I am the Lord." Jesus brought the two quotes together when he said, "Love the Lord your God with all your heart and with all your soul and with all your mind and with all your strength.' The second is this: 'Love your neighbor as yourself.' There is no commandment greater than these." (Mark 12:30, 31; cf. Matthew 22:37; Luke 10:27).

If you draw a ring with ten sections and make a commitment to stay in the center, you will see that what God has done is to offer us boundaries for our adequate protection. And if we, even with our sinful tendencies, stay within the boundaries, we will be safe. However, if we follow our natural inclinations of breaking out of the boundaries we will destroy ourselves.

May God help us to know healthy boundaries and to keep within them!

THE GREATEST GIFT OF ALL

> And now abide faith, hope, love, these three; but the greatest of these is love. (1 Corinthians 13:13 NKJV).

I do not know how much you like to receive gifts. But at varied times of the year men are expected to give gifts. I know quite a few men who have said to me that they do not mind giving gifts, but they find it hard to receive gifts. When they have to receive gifts it makes them feel too dependent. Men like to be self-sustaining, self-reliant, independent and what have you. They do not wish to feel like they owe anyone anything. Might I ask, how are you? Are you one of those men? Do you give love? Do you like to receive love?

While I struggle sometimes with the receiving of gifts, especially when it makes me feel that those who give it to me are under obligation, I have learned that in as much as I like to give gifts, I need to learn to receive gifts. Too often giving gifts can be caught up with pride, so the giver of a gift needs to stay under caution that what is being offered is graciously filled with love. Love is the greatest gift of all. Giving love and receiving love places one in vulnerable position and demands humility. When we speak of love we have to make sure it is love and not lust or some element of manipulation.

I have met people who use seduction to receive love. So I like to warn that we need to be wise in dealing with them, especially when we are in seasons of giving and receiving gifts. But we should not allow our caution to destroy our generosity and compassion. In fact, let me draw your attention to the gift from heaven. God gave to humanity the greatest gift of all, namely, the gift of Christ, which translates into the gift of life, eternal life, the gift of love, the gift of hope, the gift of grace, the gift of light, the gift(s) of the Spirit, the gift of wisdom, the gift of the cross, and the gift of the resurrection. It is my judgment that I need not take time to explain all the gifts that I have stated in the translations above, but it is important for us to learn that we need to be thankful for such gifts.

Think about what is stated in Matthew 7:11 and Luke 11:13, namely, that as evil human beings we still know how to give good gifts to our children, and how much more our heavenly Father gives good gifts to those who are willing to ask him." And think of the reality that how he has given us the gift of his Son. As is stated in John 3:16, "For God so loved the world that He gave His only begotten Son, that whoever believes in Him should not perish but have everlasting life."

Do I need say more? As ungrateful as we are, God sent his Son, the greatest gift of all. What do we need to do? Open our hearts and receive him as the greatest gift of all. It costs the best of heaven's treasure, but to us it is free.

IDOLS OF THE HEART

> You shall have no other gods before Me. (Exodus 20:3 NKJV).

It is an interesting fact how easily we turn the precious gifts God has given to us into objects of idolatry. Of course, the real issue with idolatry is not the little images that we see on the outside, but what is in our hearts. We make idols in our hearts; sometimes we bring them in the open, but in our deceptiveness we generally seek to hide them. And, of course, we tell ourselves that God cannot see them. This is why the Lord told Ezekiel to observe carefully, and then speak to the people of Israel thus:

> "Son of man, these men have set up their idols in their hearts, and put before them that which causes them to stumble into iniquity. Should I let myself be inquired of at all by them? "Therefore speak to them, and say to them, 'Thus says the Lord God: "Everyone of the house of Israel who sets up his idols in his heart, and puts before him what causes him to stumble into iniquity, and then comes to the prophet, I the Lord will answer him who comes, according to the multitude of his idols, that I may seize the house of Israel by their heart, because they are all estranged from Me by their idols."' (Ezekiel 14:3-5 NKJV).

The text is of interest, especially where it takes note that while a physical space can be filled with only a single idol, the heart has space for multiple idols. Here are ten that I consider most all-embracing.

1. The idols of consumerism- The things we accumulate to fill our empty souls.
2. The idols of egocentrism – We worship ourselves, even though our bodies.
3. The idols of ideology – We think our ideas are absolute.
4. The idols of possessions – We seek to exchange our lives for things
5. The idols of traditions - We hold to traditions instead of truth
6. The idols of lusts – We are led by our lusts instead of our love.
7. The idols of false piety – We make our religion replace our God.
8. The idols of worldliness – We fill our hearts with the fantasies of the world
9. The idols of our personal accomplishments – We revel in our achievements
10. The idols of resentfulness – We hold people in our hearts and are unforgiving.

Yes, there are multitudes of idols that might be hidden in the heart. And as stated, they are in such deceptive places, that it takes God to find them and to help us destroy them. As a couple phrases of a song says, "Break down every idol, cast out every foe. Lord wash me and I shall be whiter than snow."

What matters most takes place in the heart. How well are you guarding your heart against the entry of demons and idols?

CIRCUMCISION OF THE HEART

> And the Lord your God will circumcise your heart and the heart of your descendants, to love the Lord your God with all your heart and with all your soul, that you may live. (Deuteronomy 30:6 NKJV)

The issue of circumcision which is spoken of in the Bible seems to be rather complicated. In an effort to bring clarification the Apostle Paul dealt with the question in correspondences with his churches. One window into what is said is in Romans 9:28-29: "For a person is not a Jew who is one outwardly, and true circumcision is not something visible in the flesh. On the contrary, a person is a Jew who is one inwardly, and circumcision is of the heart—by the Spirit, not the letter, that man's praise is not from men but from God." (ESV).

Whatever the origin, circumcision was adopted from Ancient times by Abraham, as part of his covenant relationship with the divine. According to what is noted in Genesis, God told Abraham to circumcise himself, his household and his slaves as an everlasting covenant in their flesh. Those who were not circumcised were to be "cut off" from their people (Genesis 17:10-14). The practice was accepted and made the sign of belonging for all who would be part of Israel's Covenant Community. On coming out of Egyptian slavery, all males were to be circumcised if they wanted to join in the Passover celebrations (Exodus 12:43-49).

It is interesting how contentious the issue of circumcision became in the history of Israel. It is more contentious with the adoption of female circumcision in parts of the world where it is used under the pretext that it is to control sexual passion. Often enough, instead of it being used as an external sign of faith connection to God, circumcision has been used for the demonstration of male power and oppression.

As the prophets of Israel came along they often reminded the people of Israel that they should not trust in the mark of circumcision for their covenant blessings, but experience the inner reality of a circumcised heart (cf Jeremiah 4:1-4; Isaiah 43:11, 60). The Apostle Paul picked up the prophets' call as he sought to wrestle with how to help the Early Christian Church to allow the entry of Gentiles. The question the Church faced was whether Christians were obligated to be circumcised. The Jerusalem Council tried to resolve the issue, stating that the burden of circumcision was not to be placed on Gentile Christians (Acts 15:1-20). However, while the Jerusalem Council sought to resolve the issue, Judaizing Christians insisted that circumcision was the way to salvation. So, Paul offered his most passionate challenge, when he told the Galatians that he wished that in the process of carrying out the act of circumcision, the knife would slip and cut off the whole gland (Galatians 5:1-2).

In effect, what is needed in religious practice is not so much the externalities, but the circumcision of the heart. That is the cutting back of the callous skin that stops the Spirit of God from entering the heart and make it possible to be responsive to God. God wants to take away our hearts of stone, so that he can give us hearts of flesh (Ezekiel 36:26).

CULTIVATING OUR HEARTS

> A good man out of the good treasure of his heart brings forth good; and an evil man out of the evil [a]treasure of his heart brings forth evil. For out of the abundance of the heart his mouth speaks. (Luke 6:45 NKJV).

When the news came to us back to our college in Massachusetts, that one of our colleagues had died while running on a beach in New Zealand, we were very devastated. He had gone home to visit his family and was out for his daily run, since he had been preparing for the Boston Marathon, in which he had participated for many years. From all that had been known about him, he was in good health. So it was quite a shock when the news came.

Some years later, we were shocked again when it was reported that another friend of ours had died while running. He had run ahead of his wife, and when she caught up to him, she saw him on the ground, gasping for breath. By the time she was able to get him to the nearest hospital, in the car of a Good Samaritan, his heart gave out.

Both colleagues that I have reported were exercise freaks, so we were curious to know what might have gone wrong. Here is what we found, if a person is exercising (example running) and stops suddenly without cooling down, the heart can go into a shock and give out. Now we understand that heart care is not just exercising, but in learning how to bring the heart to a state of relaxation.

We take many things for granted in our daily lives. For instance, we do not recognize enough how our hearts beat. Our hearts follow a certain rhythm of beating and then resting. For older adults the normal resting heart rate is between 60-100 beats per minute (bpm). We run and run, and stress and stress, and place a lot of burdens on our hearts. We fail to follow a proper rhythm of work and rest, exercise, getting fresh air, and eating as we should. We fail to take the right vitamins and minerals to sustain the heart, as we are supposed to. We allow high cholesterol to block our veins. We forget that the free radicals in our system destroy our cells, and at the end of the day, we expect to have healthy hearts and long life.

Further, let me suggest that just going to the doctor or taking care of your heart in the physical realm is not enough. Each of us need a spiritual heart check, because it is in this realm that the free radicals of sin float around in our bodies and destroy our hearts. Such is the case when we maintain anger, hatred, unforgiveness, and all the poisonous things that destroy our spirituality.

The biblical prescription for heart preservation reads, "Keep your heart with all diligence, for out of it springs the issues of life" (Proverbs 4:23). This text is intended for us to take with seriousness, how we care for our hearts. We can't expect to enjoy life without giving **diligent** attention to heart care. According to what I have read in the dictionaries, **diligence** is one of the seven heavenly virtues, opposite sloth. And to be diligent we have to be **earnest, persistent**, and **determined**, in what we are doing.

That means we have to make sure the Spirit of God does a heart assessment for us so that we can know whether or not we are doing well.

As we run the marathon on the heavenly road, let us be careful to follow the rhythm of our hearts as God has prescribed for us.

CREATING A LEGACY OF BLESSINGS

> We will not hide them from their children, but tell to the coming generation the glorious deeds of the Lord, and his might, and the wonders that he has done. (Psalm 78:4 ESV)

After creating humankind, God's first action, recorded in Scripture, was to pronounce a blessing on them. "So God created man in his own image, in the image of God He created him; male and female He created them. God ***blessed*** them and said to them, 'Be fruitful and increase in number; fill the earth and subdue it...'" (Gen. 1:27-28). This first blessing was followed by the Sabbath blessing. "Thus the heavens and the earth, and all the host of them, were finished. 2 And on the seventh day God ended His work which He had done, and He rested on the seventh day from all His work which He had done. 3 Then God blessed the seventh day and sanctified it, because in it He rested from all His work which God had created and made." (Genesis 2:1-3 NKJV).

Following such blessings, God has willed that all human beings would become channels of blessings in the earth. Unfortunately, not everyone followed God's plan. So God called out to Abraham said to him, "Through you shall all the families of the earth be blessed." (Genesis 12:3; 18:18; 22:18). Then Abraham blessed his children. Isaac blessed his children. Jacob blessed his children and the tradition of blessing followed throughout the patriarchal generations. In Jewish families even today the Sabbath remains a time when parents bless their children.

The passing a blessing is one of the most wonderful legacies that any parent or person can share with another. That means one person can speak a blessing upon others, or pray a blessing upon others, or give a gift that brings a blessing to others. It is a blessing "to speak well of others," do conducive things to transform the welfare of others, or perform intentional acts that benefit others.

As has been noted, God is the source of all blessings. But, he has called us to be channels, or conduits or agents of his blessings to others. And let us not forget that God sends his rain upon the just as well as the unjust. Jesus said, "But I say to you, 'love your enemies, bless those who curse you, do good to those who hate you, and pray for those who spitefully use you and persecute you.'" Matthew 5:44 NKJV).

In effect, let us not wait for someone to bless us, let us bless them. Let us say something nice to them. Let us do something kind to them. Let us encourage them. Let us convey grace, love, hope, peace, truth, and compassion to them. Let us affirm them. When we say words like: "I believe in you," "God believes in you," "You are valuable." "You are so special," "You are beautiful," we are sharing a blessing. As such, we will leave the greatest legacies in life –blessing after blessing.

ABOUT THE AUTHOR

Dr. D. Robert Kennedy is the pastor of the Emmanuel Worship Center, in Alexandria, Virginia, a congregation of the Allegheny East Conference of Seventh-day Adventist. He has been in ministry practice as a pastor, Conference/Union Departmental Director, College/University professor and administrator for 47 years. He has travelled all the continents and many islands of the world, preaching, teaching and offering seminars in issues having to do with church, society, organizational management, leadership and family life issues. He has written several books and published many articles and considers this collection from his weekly opinion editorials a very special blessing for men. It is his trust that those who read might be so inspired that they will share their legacy of blessings with other men.

CPSIA information can be obtained
at www.ICGtesting.com
Printed in the USA
FFHW010400131218
49810845-54329FF

9 781732 189096